John Dobie

(Wm MacCaig — ?)

THE
SCOTTISH
YEAR

THE
SCOTTISH
YEAR

A calendar of noteworthy anniversaries
in the story of Scotland

David Murison

THE MERCAT PRESS

EDINBURGH
1982

JAMES THIN,
THE MERCAT PRESS,
55 South Bridge, Edinburgh.

ISBN 0 901824 67 4

Set in 11 on 12 point Bembo
Typeset, printed and bound in Great Britain by
Spectrum Printing Company, Leith, Edinburgh.

PREFATORY NOTE

The author has tried to range as widely and from as many aspects as possible, and to cover within feasible limits the outstanding incidents that make up the Scottish drama. But readers who will look in vain for some memorable event which they could wish had been included, are welcome to add as many of their own as they choose. Selection is endless.

There are some who wonder whether Scotland has a future; it certainly has a long past, and one that should not be forgotten.

It only remains to add that Buchan's cold periods are now treated with some reserve, and that the monthly passages from John Reid's *Scots Gard'ner* are put in for interest and not explicit instruction. No doubt views on Scottish gardening have in some respects changed since 1683.

The illustrations are from the work of
the late

AGNES MILLER PARKER, R.E., 1895-1980

Agnes Miller Parker was born at Irvine in Ayrshire in 1895. Her career started in Glasgow where she was educated at Whitehill Higher Grade School, and the Glasgow School of Art under Maurice Grieffenhagen, A.R.A., where she gained a Haldane Scholarship and later taught from 1918-20. In 1929 she was awarded the Walter Brewster Prize at the first International Exhibition of Engraving and Lithography in Chicago, and in 1930 she went to Wales to work for the Gregynog Press where she became one of the foremost practitioners in the art of wood engraving. Since then she illustrated books for the Oxford and Cambridge University Presses, Nonesuch Press, Golden Cockerel Press, Jonathan Cape, Victor Gollancz, and the Limited Editions Club of New York. Amongst her published work are editions of Caxton, Shakespeare, Spenser, Richard Jefferies, Thomas Hardy, and H. E. Bates. She died on 15th November, 1980 aged 85 years.

The illustrations in this book are reproduced by kind permission of her niece, Mrs. Ann Quickenden.

BUCHAN'S PERIODS

1st Cold Period	February 7th—10th.
2nd Cold Period	April 11th—14th.
3rd Cold Period	May 9th—14th.
4th Cold Period	June 29th—July 4th.
1st Warm Period	July 12th—15th.
5th Cold Period	August 6th—11th.
2nd Warm Period	August 12th—15th.
6th Cold Period	November 6th—12th.
3rd Warm Period	December 3rd—9th.

"The commencement of each of these more anomalous periods is subject to variation from year to year."
Alexander Buchan *Handy Book of Meteorology* (1866).

Breathes there the man, with soul so dead,
Who never to himself hath said,
This is my own, my native land!
Whose heart hath ne'er within him burn'd,
As home his footsteps he hath turn'd,
From wandering on a foreign strand!
If such there breathe, go, mark him well;
For him no minstrel raptures swell;
High though his titles, proud his name,
Boundless his wealth as wish can claim;
Despite these titles, power, and pelf,
The wretch, concentred all in self,
Living, shall forfeit fair renown,
And, doubly dying, shall go down
To the vile dust, from whence he sprung,
Unwept, unhonour'd, and unsung.

Scott *Lay of the Last Minstrel* vi. 1.

JANUARY

Prepare the grounds, soils, and manures. Fell trees for mechanical uses. Prune firrs, plant hawthorn hedges, and all trees and shrubs that lose the leaf if open weather. Also prune the more hardie and old planted. Manure the roots of trees that need. Drain excessive moisture; gather graffs ere they sprout, and near the end graff. Begin with the stone fruits. Secure choice plants as yet from cold and wet, and earth up such as the frosts uncovered.

   Feed weak bees. Also you may remove them.

   John Reid *The Scots Gard'ner* (1683).

First Monday, "Handsel Monday".

   "The first Monday of the New Year; so called because it has been the custom from time immemorial, for servants and others to ask or receive handsel on this day".

   Jamieson *Dictionary*.

   "As to holidays for recreation or merry-making, the people have only one in the year, called Handsel Monday."

   First Statistical Account I, 458.

About 11th January (31st Dec., Old Style). The Burning of the Clavie, a large tar-barrel, as part of the winter fire-festival, at Burghead.

About 18th January (24 days after Christmas, old style). The festival of Uphellyaa at Lerwick, with guising, masquerades, torchlight processions, and the burning of a Viking galley.

1st

Ne'erday. New Year observances included the keeping in of the last year's fire, first-footing, the giving of gifts, the mixing of *het-pints*, the drawing of the first water from the well, shinty, and other ball-games.

> "God send justice this land to reull and guyde
> And put away thift, reif, and oppressioun,
> That all trew folk may suirlie gang and ryde,
> Without discord had parliament and sessioun
> To gar trew folk bruik thair just possessioun
> And geve us grace, gud Lord, quhill we are heir,
> To ceis from syn repentand our transgressioun,
> And leif in joy now into this new yeir.
>
> Sir Richard Maitland *Ane Ballat maid at the yeirsmess,* 1559.

King Charles II crowned at Scone, 1651. The last coronation in Scotland.

> "Ane great pairt of the nobilitie, barones, and commissioneris of severall schyres wer convenit at the Abaycie of Scoone, erectit now in ane temporall lordschip, quhair the Kinges Majestie haid his residence for the tyme. . . Then the King, supported by the Great Constable and Marschall, and accompanyed with the Chancellour, arose from the throne and went out at a dore prepared for the purpos to a stage, and schawed himselff to the pepill without, quho clapped with thair handis, and cryed with a loud voyce a long tyme, 'God save the King'; the croun being all that tyme upone his heid."
> John Nicoll's *Diary*.

Carron Ironworks near Falkirk started by Roebuck and Garbett of Birmingham and Cadell of Cockenzie, 1760.

> "If the Works prove prosperous as we expect, some places in the Neighbourhood of the Firth of Forth will become one of the principal Seats of Iron works in Britain, not only for making Iron from the Ore into Barrs and Slit Iron, but into Nails and many other Manufactures".
> From a letter by Garbett.

Hence "carronades" for small naval guns also made here.

Glasgow Chamber of Commerce, the first in Britain, founded in 1783.

The New Lanark Twist Company founded, with Robert Owen as first manager, 1800.

> "My intention was not to be a mere manager . . . . . . but to change the conditions of the people, who, I saw, were surrounded by circumstances having an injurious influence upon the character of the entire population of New Lanark . . . When I mentioned to my friends that my intention was to commence a new system of management, on principles of justice and kindness, and gradually to abolish punishments in governing the population, they one and all smiled at my simplicity in imagining I could succeed in such a visionary scheme."
>
> R. Owen *Autobiography.*

The Scottish Railways merged in the L.M.S. and L.N.E.R., 1923.

4th

Faculty of Actuaries in Scotland constituted, 1856.

5th

Twelfth Night or Auld Yule (Christmas Old Style).

6th

Uphaliday or Epiphany. The end of the Twelve Days of Yule, "the Daft Days".

> "When Christ was reveled first to the gentiles be the starre whilk guydit the thre kingis to Bethleem."
>
> *Adam King's Calendar,* 1588.

The festivities were presided over by a person who found the bean in his portion of the cake prepared for the occasion, and was hence called the King (or Queen) of Bean.

First performance of Sir David Lyndsay's *Satyre of the Thrie Estaitis*, 1540.

> "They haif had ane enterluyde played in the feaste of the Epiphanne of our Lord laste paste before the King and Queen at Lithgowe and the hoole counsaile spirituall and temporall."
>
> Letter of Sir W. Eure to Thomas Cromwell, 21 Jan. 1540.

7th

Glasgow University founded by a bull of Pope Nicholas V, at the suit of King James II and Bishop William Turnbull, 1451.

Allan Ramsay died, 1758.

> "At Edinburgh, in an advanced age, Mr Allan Ramsay, formerly a bookseller in that city. He was well-known for his *Gentle Shepherd*; and many other poetical pieces in the Scottish dialect, which he wrote and collected."
>
> *Scots Magazine* XIX. 670.

8th

St Nathalan, died 678.

> "Nathalan is believed to have been born in the northern parts of the Scots, in ancient times, at Tullich, in the diocese of Aberdeen, a man of great sanctity and devotion, who after he had come to man's estate, and been imbued with the liberal arts, devoted himself and his wholly to divine contemplation."
>
> *Aberdeen Breviary.*

First Scottish newspaper appears, 1661.

> "Mercurius Caledonius: comprising the Affairs now in Agitation in Scotland, with a Survey of Foreign Intelligence". Edited by Thomas Sydserf.
>
> Only 9 numbers were published, the last dated 28 March 1661.

Death of the Earl of Stair, 1707. The nine of diamonds is known as "the curse of Scotland".

> "The nine of diamonds resembles the arms of the Earl of Stair

(or, on a saltire azure, nine lozenges of the first), who was hated for the part he played in bringing about the Massacre of Glencoe and the Union of 1707."

Scottish National Dictionary.

9th

St Fillan, 8th century saint who made his cell at Dundurn at the east end of Loch Earn. His bell and crozier are now in the National Museum.

"All the nicht afore the batall [Bannockburn], King Robert went to his devoit contemplation makand his orisoun to God and Sanct Phillane, quhais arme, as he belevit, set in silver, wes closit in ane cais within his palyeon."

Bellenden, *Boece* II. 391.

11th

Reconstitution of the High Court of Justiciary, the supreme criminal court in Scotland, 1671.

"That the ancient and necessar policie and custome of Justices aires and circuit courts, which upon occasion of the late troubles have bein intermitted, should be againe revived and continued."

Register of the Privy Council.

13th

St Kentigern (or Mungo), patron saint of Glasgow, died 603.

"He established his cathedral seat in a town called Glesgu, which is interpreted, The Dear Family, where he united to himself a famous and God-beloved family of servants of God, who practised abstinence, and who lived after the fashion of the primitive church under the apostles, without private property, in holy discipline and divine service."

Jocelyn *Life of St Kentigern.*

14th

The See of Glasgow confirmed as an archbishopric by a bull of Pope Innocent VIII, 1492.

"It is concludit and ordanit be oure soverane lord and his thre estatis that for the honour and gud public of the realme the sege of Glasgw be erect in ane Archbischoprik with sic previlegiis as accordis in law."

Acts of Parliament James IV, 14 Jan. 1489.

16th

The Act of Union of the Parliaments of England and Scotland ratified, 1707.

"The Estates of Parliament, considering that Articles of Union of the Kingdoms of Scotland and England were agreed on the twenty second of July One Thousand seven hundred and six years by the Commissioners nominated on behalf of this Kingdom, and Commissioners nominated on behalf of the Kingdom of England, upon full and mature deliberation upon the forsaids Articles of Union and Act of Parliament doth ratifie approve and confirm the same with the additions and explanations contained in the said Articles in manner and under the provisions aforementioned".

From the Preamble to the Act.

17th

Battle of Falkirk, 1746. Last Jacobite victory.

"All the Generals and their aid de camps were on foot, whereas they ought to have been on horseback, for Generals business in battle is more to command than to fight as common soldiers. However it is certain the Highlanders must have example shown them and that was the reason for it".

Lord Elcho *Account of the Affairs of Scotland.*

18th

The *Comet* makes her trial trip from Glasgow to Greenock, 1812.

The *Comet*, the first Scottish passenger steamboat, designed by Henry Bell, of 30 tons burden and 3 H.P. engine, was built by John Wood and Co., Port Glasgow, to ply on the Clyde three times a week "to sail by the power of air, wind, and steam." The *Comet* inaugurated the Scottish steamship-building industry.

19th

James Watt, engineer, born 1736.

"Watt, James, Son lawful to James Watt, wright in Greenock, and Agnes Muireheid, his spouse, was born the 19th and baptised the 25th."

Register of Baptisms for Greenock.

Thomas Ruddiman, born at Banff in 1674, grammarian, schoolmaster, reviewer, historian, printer, and publisher, Jacobite, librarian of the Advocates' Library, died 1757.

20th

St Fechan, Irish saint, died 664. Commemorated at St Vigeans, Arbroath, and Ecclefechan in Dumfriesshire.

21st

Death of Devorguilla, daughter of Alan, Lord of Galloway, mother of King John Baliol, foundress of Sweetheart Abbey and Baliol College, Oxford, 1290.

23rd

Lead-mining in Upper Clydesdale licensed, 1562.

"We, Johne Achisone and Johne Aslowane, burges of Edinburgh, . . . forsamekill as hir Grace hes grantit and given licence to us, oure partinaris and servandis, in our name, to wirk and wyn in the leid mynis of Glengoner and Wenlok. . ."

Register of the Great Seal.

James Stewart, Earl of Moray, Regent of Scotland, assassinated by James Hamilton of Bothwellhaugh at Linlithgow, 1570.

"The regent intended to ryde by the place suspected with speed, but was hinderd by the throng. So Bothwellhauche shott at him with a hacque-butt through a tirleis window, from a stair whereupon were hung sheetes to drie; but in truthe to hide the smooke, and mak the place the less suspected. The regent is shott a little under the navell, and neere the reins, and with the same bullet the horse upon which George Dowglas of Parkheed, base brother to the Erll of Morton, was ryding. The murtherer fled out at a posterne gate, where he mounted upon a horse which he had gottin from John Hamilton, Abbot of Arbrothe, to carie him away with speed."

D. Calderwood *Historie of the Kirk* II. 511.

25th

St Paul.

"Giff Sanct Paullis day be fair and cleir
Than salle be ane happie yeir.
Giff it chances to snaw or rain
Than salle dew all kynd of grane.
And giff the wind do flie on loft
Than wer sall vex the countrie oft.
And giff the clouds mak darke the skye
Baith nowte and foull that yeir sall die."
Kalendar of Fearn. 17th century.

Robert Burns born at Alloway, 1759.

"There was a lad was born in Kyle,
But whatna day o whatna style,
I doubt it's hardly worth my while
To be sae nice wi Robin.
  Robin was a rovin boy,
  Rantin rovin, rantin rovin,
  Robin was a rovin boy,
  Rantin rovin Robin."
Burns *There Was a Lad, i.*

James Hogg, the Ettrick Shepherd, born 1772.

"I like to write about myself; in fact, there are few things which I like better; it is so delightful to call up old reminiscences.

I am the second of four sons by the same father and mother, namely Robert Hogg and Margaret Laidlaw. My progenitors were all shepherds of this country. My father took a lease of the farms of Ettrick House and Ettrick Hall."

Hogg *Autobiography*.

The Scotsman newspaper first issue, 1817. By Charles Maclaren, William Ritchie, and John MacDiarmid.

26th

Francis, Lord Jeffrey, a founder and editor of the *Edinburgh Review*, died, 1850.

"I could not live anywhere out of Scotland. All my recollections are Scottish, and consequently all my imaginations; and though I thank God that I have as few fixed opinions as any man of my standing, yet all the elements out of which they are made have a certain national cast also."

Letter to Lord Murray, 20 Aug. 1813.

28th

King James VI signed the Confession of Faith, 1580. "The King's or Negative Confession", later incorporated into the National Covenant of 1638.

29th

Earl Haig died, 1928.

"To all ranks of the British Army in France and Flanders. With our backs to the wall and believing in the justice of our cause each one of us must fight on to the end. The safety of our homes and the freedom of mankind alike depend on the conduct of each one of us at this critical moment."

From the order of the day, 11 April 1918.

Death of James Bridie (Osborne Henry Mavor), Scotland's foremost dramatist of the 20th century, author of *The Anatomist*, *Dr Angelus*,

The Sleeping Clergyman, Daphne Laureola, The Queen's Comedy, Mr Bolfry, etc., etc., in Edinburgh, 1951.

31st

Act "for preventing wrongous imprisonment and against undue delayes in tryals", 1701. The Scottish equivalent of the English *Habeas Corpus*.

> "All Informers shall signe their Informations and no person shall hereafter be imprisoned for custody in order to tryal for any crime or offence without a warrand in writ expressing the particular cause for which he is imprisoned . . . All crimes not inferring capital punishment shall be bailable. . . And his Majesties Advocat or Procurator fiscal shall insist in the lyball and the same shall be determined by a final sentence within fourty dayes if before the Lords of Justiciary and thirty dayes if before any other Judge."
>
> Acts of Parliament William III c.6.

Prince Charles Edward Stewart died in Rome, 1788.

> "His eye brightened, his face assumed unwonted animation, and he entered upon the narrative of his Scottish campaigns with a distinct, but somewhat vehement energy of manner . . . and at length proceeded to allude to the dreadful penalties with which the chiefs among them has been visited. But here the tide of emotion rose too high to allow him to go on; his voice faltered, his eye became fixed, and he fell convulsed on the floor. The noise brought into the room his daughter, the Duchess of Albany, who happened to be in an adjoining apartment. 'Sir', she exclaimed, 'What is this? You have been speaking to my father about Scotland and the Highlanders! No one dares to mention these subjects in his presence.' "
>
> > From an account of a conversation with the Prince in Italy about 1788, by a Mr Greathead, a friend of Charles Fox.
>
> > "Soraidh bhuan dha'n t-suaithneas bhàn,
> > Gu lá-luain cha ghluais o'n bhas;
> > Ghlac an uaigh an suaithneas bàn;
> > 'S leacan fuaraidh tuaim a thàmh.

(A long farewell to the white cockade; it will not stir from death till doomsday. The grave has taken the white cockade; the cold stone is the tomb of rest)."

William Ross *Marbh-rann do Phriunssa Tearlach.*

FEBRUARY

Plant any trees or shrubs that lose the leaf, also lay such for increase;
see June.

Continue to destroy vermine.

Graffing is now in season, see the last month.

Prune all trees and shrubs except tender greens. Nail and dress
them at the wall. Cover the roots of trees layed bair the foreend of
winter, if any be. Plant hawthorn hedges, willows, etc.

Plant peas, beans, cabbage, sow parsley, spinach, marygold and
other hardy pot-herbs.

Let carnations and such sheltered flowers get air in mild weather.
But keep close the green-house.

Now you may remove bees and feed weak stocks.

John Reid *The Scots Gard'ner* (1683).

1st

The first day of Spring in the Celtic calendar.

St Bride of Kildare (died *c.* 525). She was confused with Brigit, the
Celtic goddess of Spring, and many pagan practices are associated
with her cult.

"Each day and night that I say the genealogy of Brigid, I shall
not be killed, I shall not be robbed, I shall not be put in

prison, I shall not be bewitched, nor will Christ omit to protect me."

A. Carmichael *Carmina Gadelica* I. 175.

Alexander Selkirk found, 1709, on the island of Juan Fernandez where he had lived alone since October 1704. Born in Largo in 1676, he was the original of Defoe's *Robinson Crusoe*.

"The Duke's Boat went ashore and found one Alexander Selkirk. He was clothed in a Goat-skin Jacket, Breeches, and Cap, sewed together with thongs of the same. Only Captain Fry bore him Company to his Habitation. Having with much difficulty climbed up and crept down many Rocks he came at last into a pleasant Spot of Ground, full of Grass and furnished with Trees, where he saw two small Huts indifferently built, the one being the Lodging-Room, and the other the Kitchen. Mr Fry saw likewise his Kettle, Spit, Bedstead, and Goatskin bed, and a Number of tame goats about his Habitation."

Edward Cook *A Voyage to the South Sea* (1712).

The Highland Railway formed by the amalgamation of the Inverness and Perth Junction and the Inverness and Aberdeen Junction Railways, 1865.

Partridge and pheasant shooting ends.

2nd

Candlemas. The Purification of the Virgin. The first of the Scottish quarter days. Gifts used to be made to schoolmasters by their pupils on this day.

Weather Lore:

"If Candlemas day be dry and fair,
The half o the winter's to come and mair;
If Candlemas day be wet and foul,
The half o the winter's gane at Yule."

North-East Calendar rhyme:

"First comes Cannlemas and syne the new meen,

The neist Tyesday efter that is Festern's Een;
That meen out and the neist meen's hicht,
And the neist Sunday efter that's aye Pace richt."

A day of pageants and religious plays in mediaeval Scotland:
"The provest and baillies statut and ordanit that the said
craftsmen and thair successoris sal in order to the Offering in
the Play pass twa and twa togedir socialie; in the first the
flescheris, barbouris, baxteris, cordinaris, skineris, couparis,
wrichtis, hatmakaris, and bonatmakaris togider; walcaris,
litstaris, wobstaris, tailyeouris, goldsmiths, blaksmithis, and
hammermen; and the craftsmen sal furnyss the Pageants."
Burgh Records of Aberdeen, 30 January 1505.

King James I married Lady Jane Beaufort, daughter of the Earl of
Somerset, in the Church of St Mary Overy, Southwark, 1424. He
saw her first from his prison window:
"And therewith kest I doune myn eye ageyne,
Quhare as I sawe walking under the toure,
Full secretly, new cummyn hir to pleyne,
The fairest and the freschest yonge floure
That ever I sawe, me thoght, before that houre;
For quhich sodayn abate anon astert
The blude of all my body to my hert."
King James *The Kingis Quair* xl.

Battle of Inverlochy, between Royalists and Covenanters, 1645.
"The difficultest march of all was over the Lochaber
mountains, which we at last surmounted, and came upon the
back of the enemy when they least expected us. . . There were
at least fifteen hundred killed in the battle and the pursuit,
among whom there are a great many of the most considerable
gentleman of the name of Campbell, and some of them nearly
related to the Earl of Argyll."
Marquis of Montrose to King Charles I, 3rd Feb. 1645.

"Chunna' mi 'n t-arm a dol an ordugh,
'S bha buaidh an là le Clann-Domhnuill."
(I saw the army marching in order
And victory that day was with Clan Donald).
John MacDonald of Keppoch (Iain Lom)
Latha Inbhir-Lochaidh.

James Chalmers, deviser of the adhesive postage stamp, born in Arbroath, 1782. The stamp first appeared in 1838.

Socialist Sunday Schools started in Glasgow, 1896.
"Precept 3. Make every day holy by good and useful deeds and kindly actions.
Precept 9. Do not think that those who love their own country must hate and despise other nations, or wish for war, which is a remnant of barbarism.
Precept 10. Look forward to the day when all men and women will be free citizens of one fatherland and live together as brothers and sisters in peace and righteousness."

Fastern's Een (Shrove Tuesday), Bannock Nicht, the first Tuesday after the Candlemas new moon, formerly celebrated by the baking of bannocks of oatmeal and eggs with various articles of divination, ring, button, thimble, etc., and by cock-fighting, street foot- and hand-ball.

4th

Prince James Francis Stewart (James VIII) left Scotland, 1716.
"Montrose, 4th February 1716.
It was with the view of delivering this my ancient Kingdom from the hardships it lies under and restoring it to its former happiness and independency that brought me into this country; and all the hopes of effectuating that at this time being taken from me I have been reduced much against my inclination, but by a cruel necessity, to leave the kingdom."
James VIII *Letter of Adieu to the Scotch.*

Charles II proclaimed king in Edinburgh, 1649.
"We proclaimed on Monday last the Prince King of Brittaine, France, and Ireland. . . The first necessare and prime one (as all here without exception conceive) doth put his Majestie and his people both in a hopeful proceeding; and his Majestie's

joyning with us in the Nationall Covenant, subscribed by his grandfather King James, and the Solemne League and Covenant, wherein all the well-affected of the three kingdoms are entered, and must live and die in, upon all hazards; if his Majestie may be moved to joyn with us in this one point, he will have all Scotland readie to sacrifice their lives for his service."

> Letter of Robert Baillie to William Spang, minister of the Scots Kirk at Veere in the Netherlands, 7th Feb. 1649.

William Cullen, M.D., Professor of Medicine and Chemistry in the Universities of Glasgow and Edinburgh, died 1790.

"In all our reasonings we are apter to be led into error by assuming false premises, than by drawing fallacious conclusions when the premises are just. We must therefore in our Chymical enquiries be remarkably accurate in collecting facts, as it is from these alone that a proper system can be deduced... Those facts that are merely deduced from Theory without the concurrence of Experiment ought not to be admitted. . . In relating facts every concurrent Circumstance ought to be taken notice of in order to render them as complete as possible. This is a thing of the utmost consequence and in general very little attended to."

> From his lectures.

Thomas Carlyle, historian, essayist and philosopher, died in Chelsea, 1881.

"In our wild Seer, shaggy, unkempt, like a Baptist living on locusts and wild honey, there is an untutored energy, a silent, as it were unconscious, strength, which, except in the higher walks of Literature, must be rare. Many a deep glance, and often with unspeakable precision, has he cast into mysterious Nature, and the still more mysterious Life of Man. Wonderful it is with what cutting words, now and then, he severs asunder the confusion; shears down, were it furlongs deep, into the true centre of the matter; and there not only hits the nail on the head, but with crushing force smites it home and buries it. On the other hand, let us be free to admit, he is the most unequal writer breathing. Often after some such feat, he will play truant for long pages, and go dawdling and dreaming, and mumbling and maundering the merest commonplaces, as if he were asleep with eyes open, which indeed he is."

Thomas Carlyle on Professor Teufelsdroeckh in
Sartor Resartus I. iv.

6th

St Baldred, hermit of the Bass Rock, Christian evangelist in East Lothian, died, 608.

The Earl of Moray murdered by the Earl of Huntly at Donibristle, 1592.
"Ye Hielands and ye Lawlands, O whaur hae ye been?
They hae slain the Earl o Murray And hae laid him on the green,
He was a braw gallant And he raid at the ring,
And the bonnie Earl o Murray, O, he micht hae been the King."
From the ballad on the murder.

James Leslie Mitchell (Lewis Grassic Gibbon), author of *Spartacus, A Scots Quair, Niger, The Conquest of the Maya,* etc., died 1935.
"This man set the flame of his native genius
Under the cumbering whin of the untilled field;
Lit a fire in the Mearns to illumine Scotland,
Clearing the sullen soil for a richer yield."
Helen B. Cruickshank *Spring in the Mearns.*

Execution of Mary, Queen of Scots, at Fotheringhay Castle, 1587.
"Then the said Queen kneeled downe upon the cushion, at which time, and very resolutely, and without anie token of feare she spake aloude this psalme in lattin: *In te domine confido, ne confundar in eternum* . . .
Then she laide herself upon the blocke most quietlie, and stretching out her armes and legges cryed out *In manus tuas domine* three or foure times and at the laste while one of the executioners helde her slightlie with one of his handes, the other gave her two strookes with an axe before he cutt off her head."
From Richard Wingfield's narrative.

9th

The Highland and Agricultural Society of Scotland formed in Fortune's Tontine Tavern in Edinburgh, 1784. Objects defined on 11th January 1785:

"1. An enquiry into the present state of the Highlands and Islands of Scotland, and the condition of their inhabitants.

2. An enquiry into the means of improvement of the Highlands by establishing towns and villages; by facilitating communication through different parts of the Highlands of Scotland; by roads and bridges, advancing agriculture and extending fisheries, introducing useful trades and manufactures; and by an exertion to unite the efforts of the proprietors, and call the attention of the Government towards the encouragement and production of these beneficial purposes.

The Society shall also pay a proper attention to the preservation of the language, poetry, and music of the Highlands."

10th

Murder of the Red Comyn by Robert the Bruce in the Greyfriars' Monastery, Dumfries, 1306. Later legends accrued to the story.

"That Bruce drew his dagger and stabbed Comyn is certain. Rushing to the door of the church, Bruce met two powerful barons, Kirkpatrick of Closeburn and James de Lindsay, who eagerly asked him what tidings? 'Bad tidings', answered Bruce, 'I doubt I have slain Comyn'. 'Doubtest thou?' said Kirkpatrick, 'I mak sicker!' With these words, he and Lindsay rushed into the church and despatched the wounded Comyn. The Kirkpatricks of Closeburn assumed, in memory of this deed, a hand holding a dagger, with the memorable words, 'I mak sicker'."

Scott *Lord of the Isles*. Note 12.

Bull from Pope Alexander VI to confirm the foundation of the University of Aberdeen, 1495.

"Because in the northerly parts of the kingdom there are some places separated from the rest of the realm by arms of the sea and very steep mountains, in which regions dwell men who are uncultivated, and ignorant of letters and almost wild ... the king has caused us to be humbly petitioned that there be henceforth, to flourish in all time coming, a University of general study, as well in theology and canon and civil law, and medicine and the liberal arts, as in every other lawful faculty, as at Paris and Bologna and any other universities so privileged."

From the original bull.

Henry, Lord Darnley, murdered in Kirk o' Field, Edinburgh, 1567.

"Thereafter the Erle of Bothwell came to the back yard and the said Hepburn lichtit the lunt. And my lord said thir words, 'I will nocht gang away till I see it done'; and within ane schort space it fyrit; and when they saw the house rising, and heard the crack, they ran their way."

From depositions at the Earl of Bothwell's trial, 1567.

The 4th Duke of Gordon authorised to raise the Gordon Highlanders, 1794.

"The Duchess's recruits were proud of being enlisted by one who was the greatest lady in their world, and it is natural they should have boasted of the fact, when in after years one of them was wounded, a Highland comrade would cry, 'Och cha n'eil ach pog eile o'n Bhan-Diuc'."*

C.G. Gardyne *The Life of a Regiment* II.

*"Och, that's but another kiss from the Duchess", in allusion to the story that each recruit took his shilling from the Duchess's lips.

Rockall formally incorporated into Scotland, 1972. Uninhabited, about 290 miles from the mainland, it had been annexed by a boarding party from H.M.S. *Vidal* in 1955.

12th

Rev. Henry Duncan, minister of Ruthwell, founder of the "Dumfries and Galloway Courier", restorer of the Ruthwell Cross erected about 730, and promoter of the first savings bank in 1810, died, 1846.

13th

Kenneth MacAlpin, first King of Scots, died at Forteviot, 858.

"On whom this verse was composed:
That Kenneth with endless studs of horses lives not,
Causes weeping in every house.
There is not a king of his renown under heaven
Right to the heart of Rome'."
Irish Annals of MacFirbis, Year 858.

Massacre of Glencoe, 1692.

"You are hereby ordered to fall upon the Rebels, the MacDonalds of Glenco, and put all to the Sword under 70. You are to have especial care that the Old Fox and his Sons do upon no account escape your Hands; You are to secure all the Avenues that no Man escape: This you are to put in Execution at five a clock in the Morning precisely. This is by the King's special Command for the Good and Safety of the Country, that these miscreants may be cut off, Root and Branch."
Major Robert Duncanson to Captain Robert Campbell of Glenlyon.

William Burness died at Lochlea, 1784. His son wrote his epitaph:

"The pitying Heart that felt for human Woe;
The dauntless heart that fear'd no human Pride;
The Friend of Man, to vice alone a foe;
for 'ev'n his failings lean'd to Virtue's side'."
From his tombstone in Alloway Churchyard.

Scottish Youth Hostel Association formed, 1931.

14th

St Valentine's Day.
"Yestreen at the valentines' dealing,
My heart to my mou' gied a sten';

> For thrice I drew ane without failing,
> And thrice it was written—Tam Glen."
> Burns *Tam Glen*.

"Tomorrow is St Valentine's Day, when every bird chooses her mate. I will plague you no longer now, providing you will let me see you from your window tomorrow when the sun first peeps over the eastern hill, and give me right to be your Valentine for the year."

Scott *The Fair Maid of Perth* ii.

15th

Caledonian Railway opened, 1848.

17th

A Gipsy Kingdom recognised in Scotland by King James V, 1540.

"James, be the grace of God King of Scottis, to oure Shireffis, &c., Greting: Forsamekill as it is humlie menit and schewin to us be oure lovit Johnne Faw, lord and erle of Litill Egipt, that quhair he obtenit oure Lettres under oure Grete Seile direct to yow all and sundry oure saidis Shireffis, &c. havand autoritie within oure realme to assist to him in execution of justice upon his cumpany and folkis conforme to the lawis of Egipt, and in punissing of all thame that rebellis aganis him".

From the writ of the Privy Council.

James MacPherson, author of *Fragments of Ancient Poetry, Collected in the Highlands of Scotland and translated from the Gaelic or Erse Language*—the Ossianic poems—died at Kingussie, 1796.

"Autumn is dark on the mountains; grey mist rests on the hills. The whirlwind is heard on the heath. Dark rolls the river through the narrow plain. A tree stands alone on the hill and marks the grave of Connal. The leaves whirl round with the wind, and strew the grave of the dead."

From Fragment V, *Connal and Crimora*.

18th

St Colman, 7th century. As bishop of Lindisfarne, he championed the cause of the Celtic Church against the Church of Rome at the Synod of Whitby, 664.

20th

Murder of the Earl of Douglas by James II, 1452.

"He send for the Earl of Douglas and callit for him werie humblie to Striveling to come and speik with him, and thair efter callit him to the supper and bankitit him werie reallie, thinkand gif it might be possibill ether with gentillness or goode deid to draw him fre his attempt that he porpossit to do . . . And sa he pullit fourth ane suord and said, "I sie weill, my Lord, my prayer can do nothing to cause yow desist frome your wickit consallouris," and thair efter immedeatlie strak him throw the body with the suord, and thair efter the gaird heirand of the tumult within the challmer ruschit and slew the Earle out of hand."

Pitscottie *Croniclis* XVIII. xx.

Orkney and Shetland annexed to the crown of Scotland as security for the dowry of Princess Margaret, daughter of Christian I, King of Norway and Denmark, and wife of James III of Scotland, 1472.

"Alsua the samyn day our souerain lorde, with deliverance of his thre estatis, annext and uniit the erledome of Orkney and the lordschip of Scheteland to the croun, nocht to be gevin away in tyme to cum to na persoune nor persounis except anerly til ane of the kingis sonis of lachful bed."

Acts of Parliament James III.

21st

King James I assassinated by Sir Robert Graham in the Blackfriars Monastery, Perth, 1437.

"And then the kyng cryed hym mercy, 'Thow cruell tirant', quod Grame to hym, 'thow hadest nevyr mercy of lordes borne of thy blode, ne of non other gentilman that came yn thy daunger, therfor no mercy shalt thow have here'. Thane said the kyng, 'I besech the that for the salvacion of my soule, ye woll let me have a confessore'. Quod the said Grame, 'Thow shalt never have other confessore bot this same sword'."

> The Dethe of the King of Scotis translated from the Latin
> by John Shirley.

22nd

Death of Adam Ferguson, born at Logierait 1723, Chaplain in the Black Watch, Professor of Moral Philosophy at Edinburgh, forerunner of modern sociology, author of Essay on the History of Civil Society, Principles of Moral and Political Science, etc., 1813.

"Yet one property by which man is distinguished has been sometimes overlooked in the account of his nature, or has only served to mislead our attention. In other classes of animals, the individual advances from infancy to age or maturity; and he attains, in the compass of a single life, to all the perfection his nature can reach; but in the human kind, the species has a progress as well as the individual; they build in every subsequent age on foundations formerly laid; and in a succession of years tend to a perfection in the application of their faculties, to which the aid of long experience is required, and to which many generations must have combined their endeavours."

> Essay on the History of Civil Society (1767) I. i.

23rd

St Boisil, Prior of Melrose, Confessor, died, 664.

"Cuthbert first entered into the monastery of Melrose, on which was placed Boisil, a priest of great virtue and of a prophetic spirit. . . Boisil was standing before the doors of the monastery and saw him first. Foreseeing in spirit what an illustrious man the stranger would become, he made this single remark to the bystanders, 'Behold a servant of the Lord!' "

> Bede Ecclesiastical History IV. xxvii., Life of
> St Cuthbert vi.

Declaration of the Clergy and People in favour of King Robert Bruce from the Church of the Friars Minor in Dundee, 1310.

"With the concurrence and consent of the said people he was chosen to be king, that he might reform the deformities of the kingdom, correct what required correction, and direct what needed direction; and having been by their authority set over the kingdom, he was solemnly made King of Scots, and with him the faithful people of the kingdom will live and die."

From the Latin original in the Register House, Edinburgh.

25th

William Buchan, M.D., born at Ancrum, author of *Domestic Medicine*, died in London, 1805.

"Domestic Medicine: or The Family Physician, being an attempt to render the Medical Art more generally useful, by showing people what is in their own power, both with respect to the prevention and cure of diseases; chiefly calculated to recommend a proper attention to regimen and simple medicines.   Edinburgh, 1769."

Perhaps the world's best seller in popular medicine books.

26th

Naturalisation granted to Philip van der Straten, a Fleming settled in Kelso, where he had set up a woollen manufactory, the beginning of the Border woollen industry, 1672.

"Anent a petition presented by Philippus van der Straten. . . intending to reseid in this country and imploy a considerable stock of money in dressing and refining of wooll, in order to which he hath already sett up a work and imployed diverse workmen who are now refyning and dressing of Scottes wooll at Kelso. . . being born in Bruges in Flanders."

Register of the Privy Council.

27th

Battle of Ancrum. The Scots under the Earl of Angus defeated the

English under Sir Ralph Eure, 1545.

"As the Scots began to charge, the Earl of Angus, seeing a heron arise out of the marsh, cried out, 'Oh that I had my white hawk here, that we might all join battle at once!' The English, surprised and out of breath, and having besides the wind in their face, which blew the smoke of the gunpowder, and the sun in their eyes, were completely defeated and compelled to take to flight. . . Tradition says that a beautiful young maiden, called Lillyard, followed her lover from the little village of Maxton, and when she saw him fall in battle, rushed herself into the heart of the fight and was killed, after slaying several of the English."

Scott *Tales of a Grandfather* xxix.

28th

St Andrews University founded by Bishop Wardlaw, 1412.

"Henry by divine permission Bishop of St Andrews, of our lord the Pope and of the Apostolic See legate, with full power throughout the kingdom of Scotland specially constituted, to venerable men, the doctors, masters, bachelors and all scholars dwelling in our city of St Andrews, present dwelling and to come, greeting, with the divine blessing— . . . whereby your University instituted and founded in fact by us and by you under favour of the divine mercy now laudably commenced..."

From the bull of Pope Benedict XIII confirming Wardlaw's Charter.

The National Covenant subscribed in Greyfriars Church, Edinburgh, 1638.

"The Confession of Faith, subscribed at first by the King's Majestie and his houshold in the year of God 1580, thereafter by persons of all ranks anno 1581, by ordinance of the Lords of the Secret Counsell, and Acts of the General Assembly, with a generall bond for maintenance of the true religion, and the king's person, and now subscribed anno 1638 by us noblemen, barons, gentlemen, burgesses, ministers and commons under-subscribing together with our resolution and promises for the causes afterspecified to maintaine the said true religion, and the King's Majestie according to the Confession foresayd and acts of parliament."

From the Preamble.

29th

"Leap year was ne'er a guid sheep year."
Scottish farmers' rhyme.

Patrick Hamilton, student of Paris, Louvain, St Andrews, Marburg, Abbot of Fearn, burned at St Andrews for heresy, the first Reformation martyr in Scotland, 1528.

"A meary gentillman, named Johnne Lyndesay, famylliar to Bischope James Betoun, standing by when consultatioun was had, said, 'My Lord, yf ye burne any mo, except ye follow my counsall, ye will utterlye destroy your selves. Yf ye will burne thame, lett thame be brunt in low sellaris; for the reik of Maister Patrik Hammyltoun hes infected as many as it blew upoun."

John Knox *History of the Reformation* I. 42.

MARCH

Re-delve, mix and rake your ground for immediate use. Delve about the roots of all your trees. Yet plant trees and other greens. Also prune such except resinous. Propagate by laying, circumposition, and especially by cuttings. Sow the seeds of most trees and hardy greens. Delve down the manures that lay about your young trees all winter, covering on litter again topped with earth to prevent drought in summer: this is a material observation and more especially for such as are late planted. Slit the bark of ill-thriving trees. Graffing is yet in season (but too late for stone fruit), cut off the heads of them inoculated.

Set peas, beans, cabbage, asparagus. Sow parsley, beets, succory, sellery. Plant shallot, garleeks, potatoes. Sow onions, lettuce, cresses, parsneep, radish, etc. And on the hot-bed coleflower, and if you please, cucumber, etc.

Slip and set July-flowers, and other fibrous-rooted flowers. Be careful of the tender plants; the piercing colds are now on foot. Turne your fruit in the room but open not yet the windows.

Catch moles, mice, snails, worms, frogs' spawn.

Half open passages for bees, they begin to flit; keep them close night and morning; yet you may remove them.

John Reid *The Scots Gard'ner* (1683).

St Ernan or Ernoc (Mo Ernoc), patron saint of Kilmarnock, died, 625.

St Monan, with dedications in Fife, 7th century.

George Wishart, Protestant martyr, burned at the stake in St Andrews, 1546.

> "Last of all, the hangman, that was his tormentor, sat down upon his knees, and said, 'Sir, I pray you, forgive me for I am not guilty of your death.' To whom he answered, 'Come hither to me.' When he was come to him, he kissed his cheek and said, 'Lo! here is a token that I forgive thee. My heart, do thy office.'
>
> John Knox *History of the Reformation* I. 171.

The Advocates' Library, since 1925 the National Library of Scotland, opened by Sir George Mackenzie, the Lord Advocate, its founder, 1682.

Death of Neil Gow, born at Inver near Dunkeld, 1727, Scotland's most famous fiddler of the national dance music, 1807.

> "You've surely heard o' famous Niel, The man that played the fiddle weel,
> I wat he was a canty chiel, And dearly loved the whisky, O,
> And aye sin he wore tartan hose, He dearly loved the Athole brose,
> And wae was he, ye may suppose, To bid fareweel to whisky, O."
>
> From a song by Miss Agnes Lyon of Glamis to Gow's tune "Fareweel to Whisky".

Referendum on the Scottish Devolution Bill, 1979.

> Result: For the proposals—1,230,937 (32.85%).
> Against the proposals—1,153,503 (30.78%).
> Majority for—77,435.
> 6 Regions voted for, 6 voted against.
> 36.37% did not vote.

Shooting of game birds ends.

Whuppitie Stourie celebrated at Lanark, when the advent of spring is hailed by the local youth engaging in battle with the youth of New Lanark.

2nd

King Robert II, first of the House of Stewart, born at Renfrew, 1316.
"Marjorie Bruce, daughter of the renowned Robert I and wife of Walter, Great Stewart of Scotland, at that time lord of this country, being hunting at this place, was thrown from her horse, and by the fall, suffered a dislocation of the vertebrae of her neck, and died on the spot. She, being pregnant, fell in labour of King Robert II."
G. Crawfurd *Genealogical History of the Stewarts* (1710).

The Clydesdale Bank founded, 1838.
"The Clydesdale Banking Company. Capital, One Million. Under the above designation, it is proposed to establish a New Joint-Stock Banking Company in the City of Glasgow, on principles which will enable the Capitalist, Merchant, Manufacturer, and Tradesman to participate in the benefits of banking operations."
From the original prospectus.

3rd

Death of Robert Adam, architect, 1792.
Born at Kirkcaldy, 1728, with his brothers James, John, and William, he was responsible for many public and private buildings in the Neo-Classical style, with decorations and furnishings to match, e.g. Dumfries House, the Register House, the Old College, Charlotte Square, Edinburgh, and in England at Harewood, Syon, Osterley, Fitzroy Square and the Adelphi, London, Architect of the King's Works, 1761, buried in Westminster Abbey.

4th

The Forth Railway Bridge opened for traffic, 1890.

> Total length: 1 mile 1005 yards. Main spans: 1710 feet long, the track 156 feet above high water, the cantilever towers 361 feet high. Designed by Sir John Fowler and Sir Benjamin Baker.

5th

Death of Flora MacDonald at Kilmuir in Skye, 1790.

> "She effected the escape of Prince Charles Edward from South Uist after the battle of Culloden in 1746, and in 1779, when returning from America on board a ship attacked by a French privateer, encouraged the sailors to make a spirited and successful resistance, thus risking her life for both the Houses of Stuart and Hanover."
>
> From her memorial window in St Columba's Church, Portree.

6th

St Baldred, hermit of the Bass Rock, died, 608.

Act of Parliament anent target practice and military parades, and against football and golf, the first mention in Scottish history of these games, 1457.

> "It is decretyt and ordanyt that wapinschawingis be haldin be the lordis and baronys sprituale and temporale four tymis in the yeir. And that the futball and the golf be utterly cryit doune and nocht usyt. And at the bowe merkis be maide at ilk paroch kirk a paire of buttis and schuting be usyt ilk sunday."
>
> Acts of Parliament James III.

7th

Chartist Riots in Glasgow, 1848.

8th

St Duthac, Bishop of Tain (Gaelic Baile Dubhthaich), died, 1065.

David Rizzio, French Secretary to Queen Mary, murdered in Holyroodhouse, 1566.

> "The King was past up to the Queen of befoir and was leanan upoun her chair, when the Lord Ruthven entrit with his knappisca upoun his head, and George the postulat entrit in with him and dyvers uther, sa rudly and unreverently that the burd fell, the candelis and meat and plaitis fell. Signor David tok the Queen about the waist and cryit for marcy. Bot George Douglas pluckit fourth the Kingis dagger and strak him first with it, leaving it sticking within him. He geving gret skirlis and cryis, was rudly reft from the Quen, wha culd not get him saif, nother for boist nor fairnes. He wes forceably drawen fourth of the cabinet and slain in the uter hall and hir Majeste keped as captyve."
>
> Sir James Melville *Memoirs*.

Publication of "An inquiry into the Nature and Causes of the Wealth of Nations", written in Kirkcaldy by Adam Smith, 1776. The foundation of modern economics.

> "The annual labour of every nation is the fund which originally supplies it with all the necessaries and conveniencies of life which it annually consumes, and which consist always either in the immediate produce of that labour, or in what is purchased with that produce from other nations.
>
> According, therefore, as this produce, or what is purchased with it, bears a greater or smaller proportion to the number of those who are to consume it, the nation will be better or worse supplied with all the necessaries and conveniencies for which it has occasion".
>
> The opening paragraphs.

10th

St Kessog, Irish missionary in the Lennox and south of Perthshire, killed, 560. His name was once a battle-cry in Scotland.

St John Ogilvie, the only Roman Catholic martyr in Scotland, put to

death, 1617, for refusing to renounce the supremacy of the Pope.
Canonized in 1976.

11th

Sir Alexander Fleming, born near Darvel, 1881, discoverer of
penicillin, 1928, Nobel prize-winner in 1945, died, 1955.

12th

Poor Advocate appointed, 1424.

> "Gif thar be ony pur creatur that for defalt of cunnyng or
> dispense can nocht or may nocht folow his cause, the king for
> the lufe of God sall ordaine that the juge before quham the
> cause suld be determyt purvay and get a lele and a wyse
> advocate to folow sic pur creaturis cause and gif sic cause be
> obtenyt the wranger sall assyth bath the party scathit and the
> advocatis costis and travale."
>
> Acts of Parliament, 2 James I, c. 45.

13th

The Church in Scotland declared independent of the see of York by
Pope Clement III, 1188. Some ascribe this to Pope Celestine III, 1192.

> "For this cause, considering the reverence and devotion which
> we know thou hast had from times long ago for the Roman
> Church, we have thought fit to decree that the Scottish church
> owes subjection only to the apostolic see, whose spiritual
> daughter she is, with mediation of none."
>
> From the Latin of the bull.

John Barbour, student of Oxford and Paris, Auditor of Exchequer,
Archdeacon of Aberdeen, author of the *Brus*, died, 1395.

> "A! Fredome is a noble thing!
> Fredome mayss man to haiff liking;
> Fredome all solace to man giffis,
> He levys at es that frely levys.
> A noble hart may haiff nane es

Na ellys nocht that may him ples
Gyff fredome failyhe."
From the *Brus* I.

The Scottish Football Association formed, 1873. The constituent clubs
were Queen's Park, Clydesdale, Vale of Leven, Dumbreck, Third
Lanark, Eastern, and Granville Kilmarnock.

"Resolved that the clubs here represented form themselves into
an association for the promotion of football according to the
rules of the Football Association, and that the clubs connected
with this Association subscribe for a challenge cup to be played
for annually, the committee to propose the laws of the
competition."
From the official minutes.

14th

Claim of Right, 1689.
"Therefore the Estates of the Kingdom of Scotland find and
declaire that King James the Seventh being a profest papist did
assume the Regall power and acted as king without ever taking
the oath required by law, and hath by the advyce of evill and
wicked counsellors invaded the fundamentall constitution of
the Kingdom and altered it from a legall limited monarchy to
ane arbitrary despotick power and hath exercised the same to
the subversione of the protestant religion and the violation of
the laws and liberties of the Kingdome, inverting all the ends
of government, whereby he hath forfaulted the right to the
croune and the throne is become vacant."
From the proclamation of the Convention of Estates.

Close season for trout ends.

15th

Act of Parliament to print the Bible "in the vulgar toung in Inglis or
Scottis of ane gude and trew translatioun and that they sall incur na
crimes for the hefing or reding of the samyn", 1543.
"Men beganne to inquire if it was not lawfull to such as

understood no Latine, to use the Word of their salvatioun in the tongue they understood."

David Calderwood *Historie of the Kirk of Scotland* I. 156.

The act however was not carried out, and there is no Scots translation of the Bible.

Highland Clearances in Sutherland begin, 1814.

"Patrick Sellar, now or lately residing at Culmaily in the parish of Golspie, and under-factor for the Most Noble the Marquis and Marchioness of Stafford, you are indicted and accused that, albeit by the laws of this and every other well governed realm, culpable homicide, as also oppression and real injury, the wickedly and maliciously setting on fire and burning a great extent of heath and pasture, on which a number of small tenants and other poor persons maintained their cattle; the violently turning out of their habitations a number of people, especially aged, infirm, and impotent persons, and pregnant women, and cruelly depriving them of all cover or shelter, the setting on fire, burning, pulling down and demolishing the dwelling-houses, barns, kilns, mills and other buildings, and the wantonly setting on fire, burning and otherwise destroying growing corn, timber, furniture, money, and other effects . ."

From Sellar's indictment, 23 April 1816, at Inverness. Sellar was acquitted.

Glasgow Subway opened, 1886.

17th

St Patrick, patron saint of Ireland, born (it is said) near Dumbarton, c. 389. St Patrick's Day is reckoned as the end of winter.

"I bind unto myself today The strong name of the Trinity;
By incarnation of the same The Three in One and One in Three.
Of whom all nature hath creation, Eternal Father, Spirit, Word,
Praise to the Lord of my salvation, Salvation is of Christ the Lord."

From his hymn, the *Lorica* or Breastplate.

The Crofter Commission appointed, 1883.

"Whereas We have deemed it expedient that a Commission should forth-with issue to inquire into the condition of the Crofters and Cotters in the Highlands and Islands of Scotland, and all matters affecting the same, or relating thereto, now know ye that We, reposing great trust and confidence in your knowledge, discretion, and ability, have nominated, constituted and appointed you, the said Francis, Baron Napier, Sir Kenneth Smith MacKenzie, Donald Cameron of Lochiel, Charles Fraser-MacKintosh, Alexander Nicholson, and Donald MacKinnon to be our Commissioners for the purposes of the said inquiry."

From the Royal Warrant.

18th

The Earl of Leven commissioned to raise a regiment of 800 men in the Border Country to hold Edinburgh for William of Orange against the Jacobites under the Viscount of Dundee, now the King's Own Scottish Borderers, 1689.

19th

Alexander III, King of Scots, killed accidentally on the cliffs at Kinghorn, 1286. The last of the MacAlpine dynasty and the Celtic Kings of Scotland.

> "Sen Alexander our king wes deid,
> That Scotland left in luf and le,
> Away wes sons of aill and breid,
> Off wyne and walx, of gamyn and gle.
> The gold wes changeit all in leid,
> The frute falyeit on everilk tre,
> Jesu, succour and send remeid,
> That stad is in perplexite."
>
> From Wyntoun *Original Chronicle* VII. Ch. x.

The official copy of the Act of Union signed by the Scottish Chancellor, 1707.

"The independency and sovereignty of the Kingdom, both

which the Earl of Seafield so little valued, that when he, as
Chancellor, signed the engrossed exemplification of the Act of
Union, he returned it to the clerk, in the face of Parliament,

with this despising and contemning remark, 'Now there's ane end of ane old song'."
> Lockhart of Carnwath *Papers* I. 223.

20th

St Cuthbert, bishop of Lindisfarne, Confessor, died 687.

His vision on the Lammermuirs:

"One night, whilst his companions were asleep, and he himself awake and at prayer, he suddenly saw a long stream of light break through the darkness of the night, and in the midst of it a company of the heavenly host descended to the earth, and having received among them a spirit of surpassing brightness, returned without delay to their heavenly home. When the morning was come, he found that Aidan, bishop of Lindisfarne, a man of exalted piety, had ascended to the heavenly kingdom at the very moment of his vision. Immediately therefore he delivered over the sheep which he was feeding and resolved to enter a monastery."
> Bede *Life of St Cuthbert.*

Death of Sir Richard Maitland of Lethington, Lord Privy Seal, Senator of the College of Justice, poet and anthologist, 1586.

The Maitland Ms. is one of the two chief sources of mediaeval Scots poetry, 1570-85.

Duncan MacIntyre (Donnachadh Bàn), the greatest of Gaelic poets, born in Glenorchy, 1724.

"An t-urram thar gach beinn Aig Beinn-dòrain,
De na chunnaic mi fo'n ghréin, 'S i bu bhòidhche leam,
Monadh fada, réidh, Cuile 'm faighte féidh,
Soilleireachd an t-sléibh, Bha mi sonrachadh."

(Honour to Ben Doran above all mountains; of all I have seen under the sun, it is the most beautiful to me. The long smooth moorland, the nooks where the deer are found, the clearness of the mountain-side, I noted it all.)
> From his *Moladh Beinn-dorain.*

21st

The Teuchit Storm about this date, when the lapwing nests.

John Law, of Lauriston, born in Edinburgh 1671, economist and financial speculator, supporter of paper currency, founder of the Bank of France 1716, Comptroller-General of France, 1719, after the spectacular failure of his schemes for development in the Mississippi, 1720, died in poverty in Venice, 1729.

His motto: "I shall make gold out of paper."

The National Gallery of Scotland opened, 1859.

22nd

St Finian (in Welsh Gwynnen) of Moville in Ulster, evangelist in South-west Scotland, with dedications at Kilwinning and Kirkgunzeon, died, 578.

Scottish and French troops under the Earl of Buchan defeated the English forces at Baugé in Anjou, 1421.

"Now these, until the battle of Baugé, were not thought much of, but were called by the French only mutton-eaters and wine-bibbers and consumers, and of no use to the king and kingdom of France, until and up to the time that the battle of Baugé was fought chiefly by the Scots, where the whole nobility and the flower of the English chivalry fell in battle on Easter Eve during an eight days' truce and armistice agreed upon by the chiefs, the said lords of Scotland and the duke of Clarence of England, out of reverence for Christ's passion and the taking of the sacrament."

From the *Book of Pluscarden* X. ch. 25.

23rd

Free Church of Scotland settlement at New Edinburgh, later Dunedin, New Zealand, under Rev. Thomas Burns, a nephew of the poet, 1848.

24th

King James VI succeeds to the throne of England on the death of Queen Elizabeth, 1603. The news was brought by Carey who reached Holyrood on the 26th.

> "I took horse for Edinburgh. The King was newly gone to bed by the time that I knocked at the gate. I was quickly let in and carried up to the King's chamber. I kneeled by him, and saluted him by his title of England, Scotland, France, and Ireland. He gave me his hand to kiss, and bade me welcome."
> Sir Robert Carey *Memoirs.*

25th

Annunciation Day, the old legal New Year till 1599.

Robert de Brus, Earl of Annandale, crowned King of Scots at Scone in the presence of four bishops, five earls, and the people of the land by the Countess of Buchan, 1306.

Commercial Bank of Scotland officially founded in Edinburgh by John Pitcairn, Lord Cockburn, and others, 1810.

Foundation of the Scottish Trades Union Congress, 1897.

> "The Congress was not, as some imagined, got up in opposition to the British Trades Union Congress, but because they believed that if they wanted anything well done they had to do it themselves, and in doing their own work they were in some degree lightening the work of the British Congress. Then there were many questions which affected Scotland particularly, to which their English fellow unionists could not be expected to devote the amount of time and attention they deserved."
> From the speech of a delegate.

26th

James Hutton, M.D., chemist, agricultural improver, died, 1797.

In two papers presented to the Royal Society of Edinburgh in 1785 he asserted the concept that geological changes are only the result of natural processes, as water, rain, tides, volcanoes, over innumerable millenia, and stressed the igneous formation of rocks, thus laying the foundations of modern geology.

"The destruction of one continent is not brought about without the renovation of the earth in the production of another . . . The results of our present inquiry is that they find no vestige of a beginning—no prospect of an end."
From his *System of Decay and Renovation.*

Death of Jean Armour, "relict of the poet Burns", 1834.
"Of a' the airts the wind can blaw,
I dearly like the west,
For there the bonnie lassie lives,
  The lassie I lo'e best.
Though wild woods grow and rivers row,
  And mony a hill between;
Baith day and night my fancy's flight
  Is ever wi' my Jean."
Written by her husband on their honeymoon.

27th

Michael Bruce, poet, born at Kinnesswood on Lochleven, 1746.
"Hail, beauteous stranger of the wood: Attendant on the spring!
Now heav'n repairs thy rural seat, And woods thy welcome sing.

Sweet bird! thy bow'r is ever green, Thy sky is ever clear;
Thou hast no sorrow in thy song, No winter in thy year!

O could I fly, I'd fly with thee: We'd make with social wing,
Our annual visit o'er the globe, Companions of the spring."
From his *Ode to the Cuckoo.*

28th

Patent granted for sulphur and chemical manufacture, 1612.

The Scots Guards commissioned, 1642.

"Whereas the Lords of our Privy Councill of Scotland, enabled by an Act of Parliament to that purpose out of the speciall trust and confidence of the approved wisdome valour and abilities of Archibald Marquis of Argyle, have chosen and appointed the said Marquis to be chiefe comander of one Regiment of our Scottish subjects consisting of the number of fifteene hundred men more or fewer to be forthwith raysed in Our Kingdome of Scotland . . . "

From the Letters Patent under the Great Seal.

29th

The first of the three Borrowing Days, frequently a period of cold weather.

"March said to Aperill, 'I saw three hoggs on yonder hill,
And if you'll lend me dayis three I'll find a way to gar them dee.'
The first o' them was wind and weet, The neist o' them was snaw and sleet,
The third o' them was sic a freeze, It froze the birds' feet til the trees;
And when the three days were past and gane,
The silly puir hoggies cam hirplin hame."

Folk-rhyme on the weather.

The Royal Society of Edinburgh incorporated by charter, 1783.

"About the end of the year 1782 in a meeting of the Professors of the University of Edinburgh, many of whom were likewise members of the Philosophical Society, and warmly attached to its interests, a scheme was proposed by the Reverend Dr Robertson, Principal of the University, for the Establishment of a New Society on a more restricted plan, and after the model of some foreign Academies, which have for their object the cultivation of every branch of science, erudition, and taste."

From the Society's petition for a royal charter.

Death of Ewan MacLachlan, Gaelic poet, born in Lochaber in 1775, librarian at King's College, Aberdeen, translator of Homer into Gaelic, 1822.

30th

St Regulus or Rule, credited in legend with having brought relics of St Andrew to Kilrymont (now St Andrews) in Fife.

31st

The Scottish Regalia saved from Cromwell, 1652.

"I, Mr James Granger, minister at Kinneff, grant me to have in my custody the Honours of the Kingdom, viz. the croun, sceptre, and sword. For the croun and sceptre I raised the pavement-stone just before the pulpit in the night tyme and digged under it ane hole and put them in there . . . The sword again at the west end of the church; . . . and if it shall please God to call me by death before they be called for, your Ladyship will find them in that place."

Mr James Granger to the Countess Marischall at Dunnotar.

APRIL

Now Nature hangs her mantle green
　On every blooming tree,
And spreads her sheets o' daisies white
　Out o'er the grassy lea.

Now laverocks wake the merry morn,
　Aloft on dewy wing,
The merle in his noontide bower
　Makes woodland echoes ring.

The mavis mild wi' many a note
　Sings drowsy day to rest,
In love and freedom they rejoice,
　Wi' care nor thrall opprest.

> Now blooms the lily by the bank,
>   The primrose down the brae,
> The hawthorn's budding in the glen,
>   And milkwhite is the slae.

> Burns *Lament of Mary, Queen of Scots, on the
> Approach of Spring.*

Plant holly hedges and hawthorn too, if not too foreward. Ply and sheer hedges. Nail and prune wall-trees, etc. Slip and set sage, rosemary, thym, and all fibrous-rooted herbes and flowers. Uncover and dress strawberries. Plant artichocks, slip them and delve their plottes. Set cabbages, beans peas, kidnees. Sow asparagus, parsley, beets and beet-card. Set garleeks, potatoes. Sow onions, leeks, lettice, cresses, radish, carvy. And on the hot-bed, cucumbers, coleflowers, sweet marjoram, basill.

Set strawberries, violets, July-flowers, etc. Also sow the seeds of July-flowers, etc. Sow all your annuall flowers and rare plants, some requiring the hot-bed. Lay, beat, and roll gravel and grass. Fall to your mowing and weeding.

Destroy moles, mice, worms, and snails. Open the doors off your beehives, now they hatch.

John Reid *The Scots Gard'ner* (1683).

1st

April Fools' Day, in Scots *Hunt-the-Gowk,* in Gaelic *Là na cubhag.*

St Gilbert, the last pre-Reformation saint in Scotland to be canonised, Bishop of Caithness, builder of Dornoch Cathedral, died in 1245.

Blackwood's Magazine started as *Edinburgh Monthly Magazine,* 1817.

2nd

The College of New Aberdeen, founded by the Earl Marischal of Scotland, George Keith of Inverugie, now part of the University of Aberdeen, 1593.

"We desire to found at Aberdeen a public Gymnasium in the buildings formerly belonging to the Franciscans where young men may be thoroughly trained and instructed, both in the other humane arts and also in philosophy and a purer piety, under the charge of competent and learned teachers, to whom shall be given from our endowment such salaries as may be required."

From the Latin of the Foundation Charter.

"They haif said. Quhat say thai? Lat thame say".

The motto of Marischal College.

James Gregory, physician, Professor of Medicine in Edinburgh, one of a famous family of mathematicians and medical men, died, 1821.

His best known prescripition: Magnesia usta . . . gr. vi; Pulveris Rhei palmati . . . gr. ii; Pulveris Amomi Zingiberis . . . gr i. Misce. *Sig.* Magnesia and Rhubarb, J.G. (Gregory's Powder).

4th

The earliest known book printed in Scotland, 1508.

"Heir endis the maying and disport of Chaucer Imprintit in the south gait of Edinburgh be Walter Chepman and Androw Myllar the fourth day of Aprile the yhere of god MCCCCC and VIII yheris".

The colophon of the tract.

John Napier of Merchiston died, 1617.

Scotland's greatest mathematician, inventor of logarithms, 1614.

"A Description of the Admirable Table of Logarithms; with a declaration of the most plentifull, easy and speedy use thereof in both kinds of Trigonometrie, as also in all Mathematical calculations".

The Title of the English translation, 1616.

5th

James VI left Scotland for his new kingdom of England, 1603.

"This I must say for Scotland, and may truly vaunt it. Here I sit and governe it with my Pen. I write and it is done, and by a Clearke of the Councell I governe Scotland now, which others could not do by the sword."

King James to the English Parliament, 1607.

Skirmish at Bonnymuir, Falkirk, between the Radical Weavers and the Kilsyth Yeomanry and the 10th Hussars, 1820. An *agent provocateur* had lured some demonstrators out from Glasgow with the story of a universal rising of the people.

> "It was their purpose in going out to effect a change in public affairs; that the declarant did not mean the subversion of Government, but what he wanted was the restoration of the people's rights; that they wished Annual Parliaments and Election by Ballot; that the declarant conceived the people had a right to obtain what the majority of the nation applied for; and the declarant's idea was that it was the duty of a proper government to grant whatever was thus applied for."
>
> From the declaration by Andrew Hardie, one of the leaders, after his arrest.

6th

Declaration of Independence sent to Pope John XXII from the Scottish Parliament at Arbroath Abbey, 1320.

> "Him (Robert Bruce) also the Divine Providence and, according to our laws and customs which we will maintain even to the death, the succession of right and the due consent and assent of us all, have made our Prince and King; to whom as to him by whom deliverance has been wrought for our people, we for the defence of our liberty are bound both by right and by his deserts, and are determined in all things to adhere. But if he were to desist from what he has begun, wishing to subject us or our kingdom to the King of England or the English, we would immediately endeavour to expel him as our enemy and the subverter of his own rights and ours, and make another king who should be able to defend us. For so long as a hundred remain alive, we will never in any degree be subject to the dominion of the English. Since it is not for glory, riches or honour that we fight but for liberty alone which no good man loses but with his life."
>
> From the original Latin.

7th

Sir Thomas Urquhart of Cromartie knighted by King Charles I at

Whitehall, 1641. Poet, historian, and eccentric humourist, he is best known for his translation of the first three books of Rabelais. He was educated at King's College, Aberdeen, fought on the Royalist side in the Civil War, and is said to have died with laughter at the news of the Restoration in 1660.

He proposed to devise a "Universal Language".

"In this tongue there are eleven genders, wherein it exceedeth all other languages. Every word in this language, signifieth as well backward as forward, and however you invert the letters, still shall you fall upon significant words, whereby a wonderful facility is obtained in making of anagrams. As its interjections are more numerous, so are they more emphatical in their respective expression of passions, than that part of speech is in any other language whatsoever."

From his *Logopandecteision*.

9th

Execution of Simon Fraser, Lord Lovat, in London for his share in the Jacobite Rebellion, 1747.

"When his Lordship was going up the steps to the scaffold, assisted by two warders, he looked round, and seeing so many people, 'God save us', said he, 'Why should there be such a bustle about taking off an old grey head that can't get up three steps without two men to support it?"

Scots Magazine, April 1747.

10th

Birth of James V at Linlithgow Palace, 1512.

Death of Alexander Nasmyth, painter, 1840.

11th

Release of William Armstrong, a moss-trooper, from Carlisle Jail, 1596.

"And when we cam to the lower prison,
Where Willie of Kinmont he did lie,

'O, sleep ye, wake ye, Kinmont Willie,
Upon the morn that thou's to die?' . . .

'Farewell, farewell, my gude Lord Scrope!
My gude Lord Scrope, farewell!' he cried;
'I'll pay you for my lodging mail,
When first we meet on the Borderside.' "
From the *Ballad of Kinmont Willie*.

John Galt, poet, dramatist, biographer, traveller, secretary of the
Canada Company and founder of Guelph, Ontario, novelist and
author of *The Annals of the Parish, The Ayrshire Legatees, Sir Andrew
Wylie, The Provost, The Entail*, etc., born at Irvine 2 May 1779, died at
Greenock, 1839.

"Many, I am very free to allow, have vastly surpassed my
endeavours in the historical novel, but I do not think that I
have had numerous precursors in what I would call my
theoretical histories of society, limited, though they were
required by the subject, necessarily to the events of a
circumscribed locality".
Galt *Autobiography* II. 219.

The Battle of the Braes in Skye, between tenants of Lord
MacDonald threatened with eviction and a posse of police, 1882.

"The said Alex. Finlayson, Donald Nicolson, James Nicolson,
Malcolm Finlayson, and Peter MacDonald, assisted by a crowd
of people to the number of 150 or thereby, did wickedly and
feloniously attack and assault the said Angus Martin, . . by all
which or part thereof the said Angus Martin and the said Ewen
Robertson were deforced and by force prevented from
executing and discharging their duty, and from serving the said
actions and small debt summons".
From the Indictment in the Sheriff Court at Inverness.

12th

The Gowk's Storm, associated with the arrival of the cuckoo, of
about three days' duration about this date.

14th

Death of James Hepburn, Earl of Bothwell, third husband of Mary, Queen of Scots, at Dragsholm Castle in Denmark, 1575.

He had been a prisoner since 1567 and is thought to have become insane. His body is preserved in Faarevejle Church.

Colin Campbell of Glenure, "the Red Fox", shot in Appin by Donald Stewart, 1752. Campbell had been a notorious persecutor of Jacobites after Culloden.

"But just as he turned there came the shot of a firelock from higher up the hill; and with the very sound of it Glenure fell upon the road.

'Oh, I am dead!' he cried, several times over. The lawyer had caught him up and held him in his arms, the servant standing over and clasping his hands. And now the wounded man looked from one to another with scared eyes, and there was a change in his voice that went to the heart. 'Take care of yourselves', says he, 'I am dead.' "

R.L. Stevenson *Kidnapped* xvii.

Death of John MacCodrum, Gaelic satirical poet of North Uist, 1779.

16th

St Magnus Erlendsson killed, 1117, on Egilsay in Orkney though the treachery of his co-Earl Hakon. Buried in St Magnus Cathedral, Kirkwall.

"Stand in front of me and strike me hard on the head. It is not fitting for a chieftain to be beheaded like a thief. Take heart, poor fellow, I have prayed that God grant you his mercy."

Orkneyinga Saga, ch. 50.

Battle of Culloden, 1746.

"Mo chreach, armailt nam breacan
Bhith air sgaoileadh 's air sgapadh 's gach àit',
Aig fior-bhalgairean Shasuinn
Nach do ghnathaich bonn ceartais 'nan dàil;

Ged a bhuannaich iad baiteal
Cha b' ann d'an cruadal no 'n tapadh a bhà,
Ach gaoth aniar agus frasan
Thighinn a nios oirnn bhàrr machair nan Gall.

(Woe is me for the plaided troops scattered and routed everywhere at the hands of these utter foxes of England who observed no fairness at all in the conflict; though they won the battle, it was not from the courage or the skill of them but the westward wind and the rain coming down on us from the flat lands of the lowlanders.)

John Roy Stuart, Gaelic poet and soldier in the battle.

17th

St Donan, missionary in northern and western Scotland, killed by sea pirates in Eigg, 616.

The Educational Institute of Scotland founded in 1847, "to promote sound learning and advance the interests of education in Scotland".

From its Royal Charter, § 4.

19th

Followers of the Covenanter Richard Cameron, who had assembled at Edinburgh to guard the Revolution Convention of Estates, formed into a regiment under the Earl of Angus, 1689. Following the practice of the coventicles the regiment posted pickets before divine service and bore arms into church. The Cameronians were disbanded in 1968.

Byron died at Missolonghi in Greece, 1824.

"But I am half a Scot by birth, and bred
A whole one, and my heart flies to my head,
As 'Auld Lang syne' brings Scotland one and all,
Scotch plaids, Scotch snoods, the blue hills and clear streams,
The Dee, the Don, Balgounie's brig's black wall,
All my boy-feelings, all my gentler dreams,
Of what I then dreamt, clothed in their own pall,

Like Banquo's offspring; floating past me seems
My childhood in this childishness of mine:
I care not—'tis a glimpse of 'Auld Lang Syne'."
From *Don Juan* canto x.

20th

The Scottish National Party formed by the amalgamation of the National Party of Scotland and the Scottish Party, 1934.

"The object of the Party is Self-Government for Scotland on a basis which will enable Scotland as a partner in the British Empire with the same status as England to develop its National Life to the fullest advantage."

From its first programme.

22nd

Death of Rev. Patrick Bell of Carmyllie in Angus, inventor (in 1828) of the reaping machine, 1869.

Sir Henry Campbell-Bannerman, born in Glasgow 1836, M.P. for Stirling 1868-1908, Prime Minister 1905-1908, died in 1908.

"If we are to maintain the political supremacy of the British power it can only be by conciliation and friendship; it will never be by domination and ascendancy, because the British power cannot there or elsewhere rest securely unless it rests upon the willing consent of a sympathetic and contented people."

Speech at Oxford during the Boer War, 2 March 1900.

24th

"Foirm na nurrnuidhead agas freasdal na Sacramuinteadh (agas foirceadul an chreidimh Christuidhe) (Forms of Prayer and administration of the Sacraments and catechism of the Christian faith), translated into Gaelic by Bishop John Carsewell of the Isles, 1567. The first book ever printed in Gaelic.

Warrant from the privy Council to Sir John Hepburn to raise a regiment of 1200 men to fight in the French service, 1633. The recruits came mainly from Scottish mercenaries of Gustavus Adolphus in the Thirty Years' War. The corps ultimately became the First Regiment of Foot, the Royal Scots.

26th

General Assembly Act for erecting public libraries in presbyteries, 1709.

> "The General Assembly does hereby earnestly recommend it to such of the presbyteries of this Church as have not received any of the Books sent for that end from England, to contribute amongst themselves in order to lay a Foundation for a Library at each Presbytery seat; and also endeavour to procure Collections in their several Parishes of more or less, according as their Parishioners are able and willing to give and bestow."
>
> *Acts of General Assembly* 1709, Act xi.

David Hume, philosopher, born in Edinburgh, 1711.

> "Upon the whole then it seems undeniable that nothing can bestow more merit on any human creature than the sentiment of benevolence in an eminent degree; and that a part at least of its merit arises from its tendency to promote the interests of our species, and bestow happiness on human society."
>
> From his *Enquiry concerning the Principles of Morals.*

27th

Grant by King James IV to Henry the Minstrel, author of *The Actis and Deidis of the Illustere and Vailyeand Campioun, Schir William Wallace, Knicht of Ellerslie,* 1490.

> "The saim da, at the Kingis commande, to Blinde Hary . . . xviii shillingis.
>
> From the Lord High Treasurer's Accounts.

> "Our antecessouris, that we suld of reide,
> And hald in mynde thar nobille worthi deid,
> We lat ourslide, throw werray sleuthfulnes;
> And castis us evir til uthir besynes.

Til honour ennymyis is our haile entent,
It has beyne seyne in thir tymys bywent,
Our ald ennemys cummyn of Saxonys blud,
That nevyr yeit to Scotland wald do gud."
From *Wallace* Book I.

James Bruce of Kinnaird, born 1730, British Consul at Algiers, travelled in Abyssinia to follow the course of the Nile and found the source of the Blue Nile in 1770, died, 1794.

28th

Walter Mylne burned at the stake at St Andrews for heresy, the last Protestant martyr in Scotland, 1558.

"It makis not mekill for I ame fourescoir of yeirs bygaine, thairfor be nature have nocht lang to leif, bot gif I be brunt at this tyme thair sall ane hunder ryse in the asse of my bones better nor I and sall skatter the proude pak of yow hiepocreitis that perturbis the servandis of God."
Pitscottie *Croniclis* XXII. 24.

30th

An Comunn Gaidhealach formally instituted, 1891.

MAY

In May the plesant spray upspringis;
In May the mirthful maveis singis;
   And now in May to madynnis fawis
With tymmer wechtis to trip in ringis,
   And to play upcoill with the bawis.

In May gois gallandis bring in symmer,
And trymly occupyis thair tymmer
   With 'Hunt's up' every morning plaid;
In May gois gentill wemen gymmer,
   In gardynnis grene thair grumis to glaid.

In May begynnis the golk to gaill;
In May drawis deir to doun and daill;
In May men mellis with famyny,
And ladeis meitis thair luvaris laill,
Quhen Phebus is in Gemyny.

Sen every pastyme is at plesure,
I counsale yow to mel with mesure,
And namely now, May, June and July,
Delyt nocht lang in luvaris lesure,
Bot weit your lippis and labor hully.
From Alexander Scott *Of May.*

Pull up suckers and how about the trees. Rub off unnecessary buds.
Sheer or clip hedges. Prune tender greens (not the resinous), bring
furth the housed ones refreshing and trimming them. Sow all sweet
herbs which are tender.
    Gather snails, worms, and catch moles.
    Sow lettice, cresses, turneep, radish, peas, etc. Continue weeding
and watering. Near the end watch the bees ready to swarm.
    John Reid *The Scots Gard'ner* (1683).

1st

Beltane, the day of Spring fire-festivals, maypoles, etc.; also the day
on which the cattle were driven to their summer pasture at the
shielings in the uplands.

"On May-Day in a fairy ring
We've seen them round St Anton's spring,
Frae grass the caller dewdrops wring
    To weet their een,
And water clear as crystal spring
    To synd them clean."
        Robert Fergusson *Caller Water.*

The Gab o Mey, a cold spell of a few days commonly about this
time.

The present metrical version of the Psalms came into official use in
the Kirk of Scotland, 1650.

"The Psalms of David in Meeter: Newly translated and
diligently compared with the originall Text, and former
Translations: More plaine, smooth and agreeable to the Text,
than any heretofore."
        From the Title.

"O, enter then his gates with praise,
   Approach with joy his courts unto,
Praise, laud and bless his name always,
   For it is seemly so to do."
         From Psalm c.

The Act of Union between England and Scotland came into force,
1707.
   "The two Kingdoms of Scotland and England shall upon the
first day of May next ensuing the date hereof and for ever
after be United into One Kingdom by the Name of *Great
Britain* and the Ensigns Armorial of the said United Kingdom
be such as Her Majesty shall appoint and the Crosses of St
Andrew and St George be enjoined in such manner as Her
Majesty shall think fit and used in all Flags Banners Standards
and Ensigns both at Sea and Land. ."
         Article I of the Treaty.

David Livingstone, (born at Blantyre, 1813), medical missionary,
traveller, philanthropist, died at Ilala, Central Africa, 1873.
   "For thirty years his life was spent in an unwearied effort to
evangelise the native races, to explore the undiscovered secrets,
and abolish the desolating slave trade of Central Africa, where
with his last words he wrote, 'All I can say in my solitude is,
May Heaven's rich blessing come down on every one—
American, English, Turk—who will help to heal this open sore
of the world.' "
         From his tombstone in Westminster Abbey.

3rd

Invention of the Cross Day (Ruid Day in Barland).

Murder of Archbishop James Sharp, of St Andrews, 1679.
   "They told him there was no mercy for a Judas, an enemy and
traitor to the cause of Christ. . . While thus praying on his
knees and his hands lifted up, they struck furiously at him. . .
Then falling forward, he stretched himself out and laid his
head on his arm, as if he had been to compose himself for
sleep. The place where this horrid murder was committed is

called Magus Muir, within two miles and in sight of the town of St Andrews."

> From the official narrative given in Wodrow *History of the Sufferings of the Church of Scotland.*

Death of Sir George MacKenzie of Rosehaugh, born in Dundee, 1636, M.P. for Rosshire, 1669, King's Advocate, 1677, and prosecutor of the Covenanters, founder of the Advocates' Library, in London, 1691.

> "Behind the church [Greyfriars] is the haunted mausoleum of Sir George MacKenzie, Bloody MacKenzie, Lord Advocate in the Covenanting troubles and author of some pleasing sentiments on toleration. . It was thought a high piece of prowess to knock at the Lord Advocate's mausoleum and challenge him to appear. 'Bluidy Mackenyie, come oot if ye daur!' sang the foolhardy urchins."
>
> R.L. Stevenson *Edinburgh* v.

4th

Treaty of Northampton ratified, 1328.

> "That the kingdom of Scotland, divided in all things from the kingdom of England by its right marches, as in the time of Alexander of good memory, King of Scots, shall remain for ever entire, free and at peace, without any sort of subjection, servitude, claim, or demand whatsoever.
>
> And if we, or our predecessors in past times have sought in any way any rights to the kingdom of Scotland, we renounce and abandon them by these presents to the King of Scots, his heirs and his successors."
>
> From the Latin of the treaty.

Proclamation of the Protectorate and Union with England by General Monk, 1654.

> "The Mercat Croce of Edinburgh, quhair a proclamatioun wes emittit, declarand Oliver Cromwell to be Protector of the three kingdomes. Eftir this Proclamatioun wes red, thair wes ane uther emittit, red, and proclamed that same day, anent the Unioun of Scotland to the Commounwealth of England".
>
> John Nicoll *Diary.*

5th

Posts between Edinburgh and Berwick established at Canongate Foot, Haddington and Cockburnspath, 1603. The beginning of the public postal system in Scotland.

"To appoint, constitute and plaice in townes maist commodious for that purpois betwix this and Berwick postmaisters haifing grantit unto thame allowance and standing fie for intertyning of hors for the pacquets and ar bund to serve the carriage thairof alsweiill by nicht and day."
Register of the Privy Council VI. 567.

6th

Death of Sir James Young Simpson, M.D., Professor of Midwifery at Edinburgh, the first to use chloroform as an anaesthetic, 1870.

"I had the chloroform in the house for several days before trying it, as after seeing it such a heavy unvolatile like liquid, I despaired of it and went on dreaming about others. . . . The first night we took it, Dr Duncan, Dr Keith and I tried it simultaneously and were all under the table in a minute or two."
Letter from Simpson, 14 Nov. 1847.

7th

Invasion of Scotland by the Earl of Hertford in an attempt to force the Scottish Estates to agree to the marriage of Edward, son of Henry VIII, and Mary, Queen of Scots, resulting in the burning and destruction of Border towns and abbeys and of Edinburgh, 1554. "The Rough Wooing".

9th

John MacLean, schoolmaster, labour leader, first Soviet Consul in Britain tried in the High Court in Edinburgh for sedition, 1918.

"I wish no harm to any human being, but I, as one man, am going to exercise my freedom of speech. No human being on the face of the earth, no government is going to take from me my right to speak, my right to protest against wrong, my right to do everything that is for the benefit of mankind. I am not here then as the accused; I am here as the accuser of capitalism dripping with blood from head to foot.

I am a Socialist, and have been fighting and will fight for an absolute reconstruction of society. I am proud of my conduct. I have squared my conduct with my intellect."

From his speech in his defence.

10th

Scottish Local Government Act, 1929.

"An Act to transfer to county councils and to the town councils of certain burghs in Scotland functions of existing local authorities relating to poor relief, lunacy and mental deficiency, education, public health and other matters; to amend the law relating to local government in Scotland . . . ."

From the title, Acts 19 and 20 George V. c.25.

Abolished by the Local Government (Scotland) Act 1974.

11th

Teaching began at St Andrews. 1410, later constituted as a university by Bishop Wardlaw in 1412, and confirmed by a bull of Pope Benedict XII in 1413.

"The general study of the University in the City of St Andrews of Kilrymonth in Scotland began in 1410 after the feast of Pentecost in the time of Henry of Wardlaw, bishop, and of James Biset, prior."

Bower *Scotichronicon* XV. c. xxii.

Two female Covenanters drowned at Wigtown, 1685.

"These two women, Margaret McLachland and Margaret Wilson, were brought forth to execution. They did put the old woman first into the water. . . Then they asked Margaret Wilson if she would pray for the king. She answered that she wished the salvation of all men but the damnation of none. Upon which Major Winram offered the oath of abjuration to her. She refused it saying, 'I will not. I am one of Christ's children, let me go'. And they returned her into the water, where she finished her warfare, being a virgin martyr of eighteen years of age, suffering death for her refusing to swear the oath of abjuration and hear the curates."

Penningham Kirk Session Minutes, 1711.

12th

St Comgall of Bangor in Ireland and Tiree, missionary with Columba to the Picts, late 6th century.

Rev. James Kirkwood, M.A., 1650-1708, becomes minister of Minto, 1679. The father of public libraries in Scotland. Author of the anonymous publication of 1699: "An overture for establishing of Bibliothecks in every paroch throughout this kingdom."

The Black Watch commissioned under General Wade as the Independent Companies to police the Highlands, 1725. "The Forty-twa".

"Deoch slainte an Fhreiceadain 'S àill leinn gun cheist i,
'S i an fhàilte nach beag oirnn Dhol deiseal ar chléibh. . .

Na curaidhean calma G'am buineadh bhi 'n Albainn
Feadh mhonainean garbhlaich A' sealg air na féidh."

(A drink to the health of the Watch, and a pleasure to us without reserve, Our salute is no small one to go with good omen round our breasts. . . That the brave warriors may belong to Scotland among the rugged moors to hunt the deer.)

Duncan MacIntyre *Oran do 'n T-sean Fhreiceadan Ghaidhealach.*

13th

Battle of Langside, the final defeat of Queen Mary in her attempt to regain the throne from her son and his adherents, 1568.

"The Queen beheld this conflict within half a mile distant, standing upon a hill accompanied with Lord Boyd, the Lord Fleming and the Lord Herries son, with thirty others, who seeing the Company overthrown took the way to Dumbarton, who was so near pursued that she could not take the boat that should bring her into Dumbarton, but was driven to take the way to Dumfries."

Account in State Paper Office, London.

Alexander Buchan, F.R.S.E., meteorologist, schoolmaster at Dunblane, Secretary of the Scottish Meteorological Society, founder of the Ben Nevis Observatory and scientific weather-forecasting, died, 1907.

He is best known for his 'cold periods', spells of cold weather occurring annually about certain times of the year, according to his view, though this is now doubted.

14th

Charles II proclaimed restored king at Edinburgh, 1660.

"With all solempnities requisite, by ringing of bellis, setting out of bailfyres, sounding of trumpetis, roring of cannounes, touking of drumes, dancing about the fyres, and using all uther takins of joy for the advancement and preference of their native king to his croun and native inheritance. Quhairat also thair wes much wyne spent, the spoutes of the croce ryning and venting out abundance of wyne, placed thair for that end; and the magistrates and counsell of the toun being present, drinking the kingis helth and breking numbers of glasses."

John Nicoll *Diary.*

Death of Rev. Robert Kirk, Gaelic scholar, translator of the metrical psalms, printed the Gaelic Bible, author of *The Secret Commonwealth of Elves, Faunes, and Fairies*, minister of Aberfoyle till 1692.

"After the cermony of a seeming funeral the form of the Rev. Robert Kirk appeared to a relation, and commanded him to go to Grahame of Duchray. 'Say to Duchray who is my cousin as well as your own, that I am not dead, but a captive in Fairyland: and only one chance remains for my liberation. When the posthumous child of which my wife has been delivered since my disappearance, shall be brought to baptism, I will appear in the room, when if Duchray shall throw over my head the knife or dirk which he holds in his hand, I may

be restored to society; but if this is neglected, I am lost for
ever."

Sir Walter Scott *Demonology* (1830) 165.

The Society of Golfers of St Andrews constituted, 1754. Later the
Royal and Ancient Golf Club (1834).

"The Noblemen and Gentlemen above named, being Admirers
of the Anticient and Healthfull Exercise of the Golf, and at the
same time having the Interest and prosperity of the Anticient
City of St Andrews at heart, being the Alma Mater of the Golf
did. . . contribute for a Silver Club. . . having a St Andrew
engraved on the head thereof, to be played for on the Links of
St Andrews."

From the Club Minutes.

Duncan MacIntyre (Donnchadh Bàn), gamekeeper, soldier, town-
guardsman, Gaelic poet, died in Edinburgh 1812.

"A Mhàiri bhan gur barrail thu, 'S gur barraicht' air gach seol thu,
O' n thug mi gaol cho daingean duit, 'S mi 't fharraid anns gach
comhdhail:

'S earbsach mi ad cheanaltas, 'S na fhuair mi chean' ad chòmhradh,
Nach urrainn càch do mheallach uam 'N déis do gheallaidh
dhomh-sa."

(O Mary fair, you are beyond compare, surpassing in every
way, since I have loved you so steadfastly and ask you at each
meeting, trusting in your kindness and getting delight in your
talk, that none may entice you from me after your promise to
me.)

From his *Oran Gaoil* (Love song).

15th

Whitsunday term day, the second term day of the Scottish year, next
after Candlemas.

"Ande quhen the dais of Penthecoste war fillit, all the disciplis
war togiddir in the sammin place. And suddanlie thar was
made a sound fra heven, as of a gret wynd cummand, and it
fillit al the house quhare thai sat. And diverse tonngis as fire
apperit to thame and it sat on ilk of thame. And all war fillit

with the Haligaast, and thai began to spek diverse langages, as
the Haligaast gave to thame for to spek."
          M. Nisbet *New Testament* Acts II. 1-4 (*c.* 1520).

Marriage of Mary Queen of Scots and James Hepburn, Earl of
Bothwell, in Holyroodhouse, "not with the mass but with preaching,
at ten hours afore noon", 1567.

"Bot within four dayis thaireftir, findeing opportunitie, be
ressoun we wer past secrtelie towartis Striveling to visit the
Prince our derrest sone, in oure returning he awayted us be the
way accumpaneit with a greit force, and led us with all
diligence to Dunbar. Being thair, we reprochit him. . . Albeit
we fand his doingis rude, yit wer his answer and wordis bot
gentill.

Eftir he had be thir meanis, and mony utheris, brocht us
agaitward to his intent, he partlie extorted and partlie obtenit
oure promeis to tak him to oure husband."
          The Queen's Account from her Instructions to the
          Bishop of Dunblane to the Court of France.

16th

St Brendan the Voyager, patron saint of Bute, 6th century.

Local Government (Scotland) Act (1974) came into force, 1975.
Nine regional, 53 district and 3 island area councils, elected on
May 7th 1974, now replace the 430 previously existing local
authorities, the counties and small burghs, through which the
country had come to be administered over some six centuries.

17th

The Court of Session instituted, 1532.
"By this institution of King James V the judicatory has been
ever since called the Session or College of Justice, and the
members thereof have frequently been called the Senators of
the College of Justice, or Lords of Council and Session."
          Stair *Institutes* IV. i. 22.
"The quhilk day in presens of the Kingis grace all the forsaidis

persounis ar sworne to do and minister Justice to all our
soverane lordis liegis in all causis that sall happin to cum effor
thame eftir thair conscience knawledge and undirstanding as
thai sal ansuer to God and his hieness."

From the first clause of the Constitution.

The Disruption, when over 400 ministers and many elders left the Established Church of Scotland to form the Free Church of Scotland, 1843.

"We protest that, in the circumstances in which we are placed, it is and shall be lawful for us and such other Commissioners as may concur with us, to withdraw to a separate place of meeting for the purpose of taking steps, along with all who will adhere to us, maintaining with us the Confession of Faith and Standards of the Church of Scotland as heretofore understood, for separating in an orderly way from the Establishment. . ."

From the formal protest made by the Moderator to the General Assembly.

19th

Death of Kirkpatrick MacMillan, blacksmith at Courthill in Dumfriesshire, inventor of the bicycle, 1846.

"Glasgow, June 11th 1842. On Wednesday a gentleman, who stated he came from Thornhill in Dumfriesshire, was placed at the Gorbals public bar, charged with riding along the pavement on a velocipede to the obstruction of the passage, and with having, by so doing, thrown over a child. It appeared from his statement that he had on the day previous come all the way from Old Cumnock, a distance of forty miles, bestriding the velocipede, and that he performed the journey in the space of five hours."

Newspaper account of the first bicycle in Glasgow.

20th

Battle of Dunnichen, 685. Defeat of Ecgfrith, King of Northumbria, by Brude MacBile, King of the Picts.

"From that time the hopes and power of the English began to waver and recede; for the Picts recovered their own lands which had been held by the English and the Scots who were in Britain, and some of the Britons their liberty, which they enjoy

to this day for about forty-six years."
　　Bede *Ecclesiastical History* IV. 26.

"This day Bruide fights a battle for the land of his grandfather,
　　Unless the son of God wish it otherwise, he will die in it.
Today the son of Oswy was killed in a battle with green
　　swords,
　　Although he did penance, he shall lie in Hi after his death;
This day the son of Oswy was killed, who had the black drink,
　　Christ heard our supplications, they spared Bruide the
　　　brave."
　　Riagal of Bangor from the Irish Annals.

"Parish Bank Friendly Society of Ruthwell", founded by Rev. Henry
Duncan, the beginning of Savings Banks, 1810.

21st

Execution of James Graham, Marquis of Montrose, 1650.
　　"In his doungoing from the Tolbooth to the place of
execution, he was very richly clad in fine scarlet, laid over
with rich silver lace, his hat in his hand, his golden hat band,
his bandis and cuffis exceedingly rich, his delicate whyte gloves
on his handis, his stockings of incarnet silk and his schooes
with thair ribbenes on his feet; and sarkis provided for him
with pearling about, above ten pund the elne. All these were
provided for him by his friends, and a prettie cassock put on
him upon the scaffold, wherein he was hangit."
　　John Nicoll *Diary*.

22nd

The General Assembly of the Church of Scotland meets about this
time.

24th

David I, son of Malcolm and Margaret, the first feudal king of
Scotland and benefactor of the Church, died at Carlisle, 1153.

"He biggit xv abbais in Scotland and donate thaim with sindry landis, rentis and possessions. . . And thairfor King James the First, quhen he come to his sepulture at Dunfermling said that he was ane sair sanct for the Croune, as he wald signify that he dotat the Kirk our richelie and left the Croune our pure."

John Bellenden's translation of Boece's *Chronicles*.

25th

Flitting Day

"The 25th of May, as the Whitsunday term (Old Style), is a great day in Scotland, being that on which for the most part people change their residences. The Scotch generally lease their houses by the year, and are thus at every twelve-month's end able to shift their abode."

R. Chambers *Book of Days* I. 679.

26th

Gold and silver mines in Scotland become Crown property, 1424.

"Gif any myne of golde or silver be fundyn in ony lordis landis of the realme and it may be provyt that thre halfpennys of silver may be fynit owt of the punde of leide the Lordis of Parliament consentis that sik myne be the kingis as is usuale in uthir realmys."

Acts of Parliament James I.

29th

David Beaton, Cardinal Archbishop of St Andrews, Lord High Chancellor of Scotland, murdered in his palace by a band of Reformers, 1546.

"But James Melven presenting unto him the point of the sweard said, 'Repent thee of thy former wicked lyfe, but especiallie of the schedding of the blood of that notable instrument of God, Maister George Wisharte, which albeit the flame of fyre consumed befoir men, yitt cryes it a vengeance upoun thee, and we from God ar sent to revenge it: for heir, befoir my God, I protest that neither the hetterent of thy persone, the luif of thy riches, nor the fear of any trouble thow could have done to me in particulare, moved nor movis me to stryk thee, but only becaus thow hast bein, and remanes ane obstinat ennemye against Christ Jesus and his holy Evangell.' And so he stroke him twyse or thrise trowght with a stog sweard; and so he fell, never word heard out of his mouth but, 'I am a preast, I am a preast; fy, fy, all is gone."

John Knox *History of the Reformation* I. 177.

31st

The Royal Bank of Scotland formed from a company of debenture holders of the Equivalent stock, chartered with a capital of £111,000, 1727.

The Royal Bank was the first to devise the overdraft system.

Thomas Chalmers, mathematician, preacher, moral philosopher, economist and social reformer, theologian, leader of the Disruption of 1843 in the Church of Scotland, died, 1847.

JUNE

"In middis of June, that joly sweit seasoun,
Quhen that fair Phebus with his bemis bricht
Had dryit up the dew fra daill and doun,
In ane mornyng betwix mid day and nicht
I rais and put all sleuth and sleip asyde,
And to ane wod I went allone but gyde.

Sweit wes the smell off flouris quhyte and reid,
The noyes off birdis richt delitious,
The bewis braid blomit abone my heid,
The ground growand with gresis gratious;
Off all plesance that place wes plenteous,
With sweit odouris and birdis harmony;
The morning myld; my mirth wes mair for thy.

The rosis reid arrayit rone and ryce,
The prymeros and the purpour viola;
To heir it wes ane poynt off paradice,
Sic mirth the mavis and the merle couth ma;
The blossummis blythe brak up on bank and bra;
The smell off herbis and the fowlis cry,
Contending quha suld have the victory."

Henryson *The Taill of the Lyoun and The Mous* Prologue.

Cleanse about the roots of trees, suckers and weeds; water their covered bulks especially the new planted.

Unbind graffs. Prune all wall and standard trees. Towards the end you may inoculate and also increase by circumposition.

Transplant coleflowers, coleworts, leeks, etc. in moist weather; at least water first the ground if dry.

Sow peas, radish, turneep, lettice, chervil, cresses, etc.

Destroy snails, worms, etc.

Begin to lay carnations or July-flowers; shade, support, and prune such as will blow. Water the pots and thirsty plants. Weeding and mowing is in season, and so is distillation.

Bees now swarm. Look diligently to them.

John Reid *The Scots Gard'ner* (1683).

June is especially the month of Common Ridings, the perambulations of the boundaries of various burghs, of Hawick and Lanark (Lanimer Day) during the first week, Selkirk in the second, Linlithgow on the Tuesday after the second Thursday, Peebles in the third week.

1st

Battle of Drumclog, between Covenanters attending a conventicle and the Royalist troops under Graham of Claverhouse, 1679.
> "The greatest body of all made up against my troupe; we keeped our fyr till they were within ten pace of us; they received our fyr, and advanced to shok; . . our men sustained not the shok but fell into disorder. . . I saved the standarts, but lost on the place about aight or ten men, besides wounded; but the dragoons lost many mor. This may be counted the beginning of the rebellion."
> From Claverhouse's despatch.

Death of Sir David Wilkie, artist, King's Limner in Scotland, painted in genre style after the Dutch, *Pitlessie Fair, The Reading of the Will, The Rent Day, The Penny Wedding, The Blind Fiddler,* etc., later following the models of Velasquez and Murillo in Mediterranean scenes, 1841. His burial at sea was painted by Turner.

2nd

The Regent Morton executed for complicity in the murder of Darnley, it is said by the "Maiden", a guillotine he himself had introduced to Scotland, 1581.
> "The man that brought me these news came from Edinburgh on Friday last at two of the clock, and then the said Earl of Morton was standing on the scaffold, and it is thought the accusations that were laid against him were very slender, and that he died very stoutly."
> Letter from Sir John Fraser to Sir F. Walsingham.

Dugald Buchanan, Gaelic religious poet, born in Strathyre 1716, translator of the Gaelic New Testament, died at Kinloch Rannoch, 1786.

Much of his poetry is influenced by English poets, such as Shakespeare and Milton, and includes *The Greatness of God, The Day of Judgment, The Sufferings of Christ, The Skull, Winter.*

3rd

Robert Tannahill, poet, born in Paisley, 1774.
"Robert Tannahill (1774-1810), chief of the many Paisley poets, is little more than sweetly sentimental; but his *Jessie, the Flower o Dunblane, The Braes of Balquither, The Bonnie Wood o Craigielea,* and many more, all in the same gently amorous or gently musing vein, have found a permanent place in Scottish song-books."
T.F. Henderson *Scottish Vernacular Literature* 457.

5th

"Act for abolishing of the Acts contrair the trew religion", which established Presbyterian government in the Scottish Church after the Reformation, 1592.

European Economic Community Referendum, 1975.
Scotland voted: 1,332,286   Yes
948,039   No
Majority For: 384,147. 61% voted.
Shetland and the Western Isles had majorities against.

7th

Death of Robert the Bruce at Cardross, 1379.
"I will that as soon as I shall be dead, you will take my heart from my body and have it well embalmed; you [Sir James Douglas] and those you may choose to take with you in your train, will deposit your charge in the Holy Sepulchre of our Lord, since my body cannot go there, and wherever you pass you will let it be known that you bear the heart of King Robert of Scotland."
Froissart *Chronicle* xx.

John Rennie, born at Phantassie, East Lothian, civil engineer, builder
of Waterloo, London, and Southwark Bridges, 1761.

The Carnegie Trust for the Universities of Scotland formed, 1901.
> "I, Andrew Carnegie, of New York, and of Skibo in the
> County of Sutherland, deeming it to be my duty and one of
> my highest privileges to administer the wealth which has come
> to me as a trustee on behalf of others, and entertaining the
> belief that one of the best means of my discharging that trust is
> by providing funds for improving and extending the
> opportunties for scientific study and research in the
> Universities of Scotland, my native land, and by rendering
> attendance at these Universities and the enjoyment of their
> advantages more available to the deserving and qualified youth
> of that country to whom the payment of fees might act as a
> barrier to the enjoyment of these advantages, hereby undertake
> to deliver bonds of the United States Steel Corporation of the
> aggregate value of ten million dollars to be held by the
> Trustees . . ."
> From the Deed of Trust.

8th

The Honourable Society of Improvers in the Knowledge of
Agriculture in Scotland formed in Edinburgh by over 300
landowners, 1723.
> "Considering in how low a state the Manufactures in Scotland
> are, and how much the right Husbandry and Improvement of
> Ground is neglected, partly through want of skill in those who
> make Possession thereof, and partly through want of
> Encouragement for making proper Experiments of the several
> Improvements that the different Soils in this country are
> capable of."
> From the first Resolution of the Society.
> The Society lapsed after the '45.

The Earl of Seaforth raised a regiment for the American War among
the MacKenzies and MacRaes of Ross-shire and Sutherland, 1778.
> The Seaforth Highlanders amalgamated in 1961 with the
> Camerons to form the Queen's Own Highlanders.

9th

Death of St Columba in Iona, 597.

"Diormit then raised the holy right hand of the saint that he might bless his assembled monks. And the venerable father at the same time himself moved his hand and having given them his holy benediction in this way, he immediately breathed his last. After his soul had left the tabernacle of his body, his face still continued ruddy and brightened in a wonderful way by his vision of the angels."

From the Latin of Adamnan *Life of St Columba* III. xxiv.

Death of Maitland of Lethington, Secretary of State to Mary, Queen of Scots, 1558, after the fall of Edinburgh Castle, 1573.

"Schir Williame Maitland younger of Leithingtoun, sumtyme secretar, depairtit at the plessour of God in Leith, and incontinent without any moir wes laid in leid in the bedhous of Leith; bot within a few dayes na man durst com neir for evill sar."

Diurnal of Occurrents.

10th

Death of Marie of Guise, Queen Regent of Scotland, 1560.

"Befoir hir depairting sho causit fetch to hir James Duke of Chattellarault, James Commendatare of Sanctandrois, and utheris lordis asseidgeris of Leith, and at their cuming sho exhortit thame to be faithfull and obedient subjectis to the quenis grace hir dauchter, quha promittit to doe the same; bot as thai fulfillit the said promeis thair proceidingis will testifie."

Diurnal of Occurrents.

White Rose Day, celebrated by Jacobites as the birthday of Prince James Francis Stewart, "the Old Pretender", son of James VII, in 1688.

The Battle of Glenshiel, defeat of Scottish Jacobite and Spanish troops by Hanoverian forces, 1719.

Forth and Clyde Canal started, 1768.

11th

Battle of Sauchieburn, between James III and the confederate nobles supporting his son, the king being murdered in his flight, 1488.

"The millar and his wyff harlit him into the myle and nocht knawand quhat he was bot cast him upe in ane nuke and coverit him with ane claith. The king owercame and cryit gif thair was any preist thair to mak his confessioun. The millar and his wyffe requirit of him quhat man he was. He hapnit out unhappelie and said, 'I was your king this day at morn.' Then the myllaris wyfe ran fourth and cryit for ane preist to the king. In this meane tyme ane preist was command by—sum sayis he was the lord Grayis servand—and said, 'Here am I, ane preist; quhair is the king?' The king desirit the preist to gif him his sacrament. The preist answerit, 'That sall I do haistelie' and pullit out ane quhinger and gif him foure or fyve straikis ewin to the hart."

Pitscottie Croniclis XIX. xiii.

James Gregory, professor of mathematics at St Andrews and Edinburgh, developed photometry and the theory of numbers, invented the reflecting telescope, joint discoverer with Newton and Leibnitz of the calculus, admitted a Fellow of the Royal Society, 1668.

Joseph Black (1728-99) presents his thesis for the degree of M.D. of Edinburgh University, 1754. *De humore acido a cibis orto et magnesia alba*, the effect of magnesia on indigestion.

Black was born at Bordeaux of Scottish parentage, studied at Glasgow and succeeded William Cullen his teacher, in the Chair of Chemistry at Glasgow and then at Edinburgh. He discovered the theory of latent heat and carbon dioxide.

12th

St Ternan, saint of the Mearns, 6th century. His name is preserved in Banchory-Ternan on the Dee.

Scottish Navigation Act, 1661.

"All goods or commodities whatsoever produced or shipped which shall be imported into this Kingdome or any Ilands thereto belonging in any ships or vessels that shall not truely and only belong to the natives and inhabitants thairof (except in English or Irish vessells, provyding alwayes that Scots vessells enjoy the lyke benefits of trade within the kingdomes and dominions of England and Ireland and no otherwayes) shall be lyable to double custome and pay accordinglie."

Acts of Parliament Scotland Charles II VII. 257.

13th

Act for compulsory education, 1496.

"It is statute and ordanit throw all the realme that all barronis and frehaldaris that ar of substance put thair eldest sonis and aires to the sculis fra thai be aucht or nyne yeiris of age and till remane at the gramer sculis quhill thai be competentlie foundit and have perfite latyne."

Acts of Parliament Scotland James IV.

Emancipation of colliers from servitude to coalmasters, the last vestige of serfdom in Scotland, by 39 George III c. 56, 1799.

"Whereas many colliers, coalbearers, and salters were bound for life to and transferable with the collieries and salt works where they worked . . . from and after the passing of this Act, all the Colliers in that part of Great Britain, called Scotland, who were bound Colliers at the time of passing the said Act, shall be and they are hereby declared to be free from their Servitude."

From the Preamble to the Act.

Beginning of the Strathnaver Clearances on the Sutherland estates, 1819.

"It was a Tuesday. At an early hour of that day Mr Sellar, accompanied by the Fiscal, and escorted by a strong body of constables, sheriff-officers, and others, commenced work. Their plan of operations was to clear the cottages of their inmates, giving them about half an hour to pack up and carry off their furniture and then set the cottages on fire. To this

plan they ruthlessly adhered, without the slightest regard to any obstacle that might arise while carrying out its execution."
    D. Sage *Memorabilia.*

    Sellar had been acquitted on a charge of arson and homicide in connection with an earlier eviction in 1814.

14th

Colin MacLaurin, mathematician, professor at Aberdeen and Edinburgh, continuing Newton's work on the calculus, conics, and fluxions, died, 1746.

John Logie Baird, born in Helensburgh in 1888, first exponent of television, died, 1946.
    "For the purpose of the demonstration the head of a ventriloquist's doll was manipulated as the image to be transmitted, though the human face was also reproduced. First on a receiver in the same room as the transmitter and then on a portable receiver in another room, the visitors were shown recognisable reception of the movements of the dummy head and a person speaking. The image as transmitted was faint and often blurred, but substantiated a claim that through the 'Televisor', as Mr Baird has named his apparatus, it is possible to transmit and reproduce instantly the details of movement and such things as the play of expression on the face".
    Times report of the first demonstration of television to members of the Royal Institution in London, 27 Jan. 1926.

15th

Queen Mary surrendered to the Protestant Lords at Carberry Hill, 1567.
    "For the laird of Grange was declairen unto the Quen how that they all wald honour and serve hir, sa that sche wald abandon the Erle Bodowell, wha was the mourtherer of hir awen husband; and culd not be a husband unto hir, that had bot laitly maried the Erle of Huntleis sister. Then the Quen sent again for the lard of Grange, and said to him, that gin the

lordis wald do as he had spoken to hir, sche suld put away the
Erle Bodowell and com unto them. Then he raid up again and
saw the Erle Bodowell part, and led Hir Maieste be the brydill
doun the bra 'unto the lordis, Hir Maieste was that nycht
convoyed to Edenbrough. As sche cam throw the toun, the
common people cryed out against her Maieste at the windowes
and staires, quhilk was a pitie to heir."

Sir James Melville *Memoirs*.

Thomas Campbell, tutor, poet, author of *The Pleasures of Hope, Ye
Mariners of England, Lord Ullin's Daughter, The Battle of the Baltic,
Hohenlinden*, etc., etc., Rector of Glasgow University, 1827, one of
the founders of London University, champion of Polish freedom,
died at Boulogne, 1844.

16th

Siege of Dunbar by the English raised, 1338.

"There was no other captain in command there but the
Countess of March, commonly called Black Agnes of Dunbar.
She herself, in mockery of the English, would (in the sight of
all) dust with a fair cloth the place where a stone from their
engines had struck the ramparts. . . The Earl [of Salisbury]
escaped and Black Agnes, standing on the wall, called out to
him mockingly 'Adieu, adieu, Monsieur Montagu!' And so
having seen the letters bidding him leave all and return to
England, he withdrew without ceremony taking no leave of his
hostess."

From the Latin of *Liber Pluscardensis* ix. 36.

Rev. John Skinner, poet, theologian, Episcopal minister of Longside
in Buchan, died, 1807.

"I regret, and while I live shall regret that when I was in the
north I had not the pleasure of paying a younger brother's
dutiful respect to the author of the best Scotch song ever
Scotland saw."

Letter from Burns to Skinner, Oct. 1787.

The song referred to is *Tullochgorum*.

17th

Elgin Cathedral burned by Alexander Stewart, Earl of Buchan and Ross, son of Robert II, "the Wolf of Badenoch", 1390.

Queen Mary imprisoned in Lochleven Castle by the Council of Scotland, 1567.

Charles Macintosh, chemist, born in Glasgow in 1766, patents waterproof cloth, 1823.
> "No. 4804. Process and manufacture for rendering the texture of hemp, flax, wool, cotton, silk, and also leather, paper and other substances, impervious to water and air."
> Alphabetical Index of Patents.

18th

Act appointing a Council of Trade, 1661.
> "His Majestie with advice and consent of his Estates of Parliament, have thought it necessarie that a Councill of Trade be established with power to . . . make and set down rules, acts, and ordinances for regulating, improveing and advanceing of trade, navigation, and manufactories, and to establish severall companies and impower them with such priviledges, liberties, and immunities as shall be fittest for the good of the service."
> Acts of Parliament Scotland VII. 273.

Flora MacDonald meets Prince Charles Edward in Skye, 1746.
> "In this perplexity Captain O'Neil accidentally met with Miss Funivella or Flora MacDonald, to whom he proposed assisting the Prince to make his escape, which she at last consented to, on condition the Prince would put on women's cloaths, which he complied with. She then desired they would goe to the mountain of Corradale and stay there till they heard from her, which should be soon."
> *Lyon in Mourning* I. 66.

North British Railway opened from Edinburgh to Berwick-on-Tweed, 1846.

"The enormous size of the train must be considered, consisting of 26 or 28 carriages, and, with the five locomotives and tenders, extending to nearly a furlong, or something more than one division of Princes Street. To bystanders the sight must have been extremely imposing, especially at the curvature, where the monster train was seen to bend to the right and left, and display the flexibility of a silken cord, while rivalling the eagle's flight in speed."

From *The Scotsman* account.

19th

Birth of King James VI in Edinburgh Castle, 1566.

"Then she spoke to Sir William Stainley, 'This (sayes she) is the sone whome I hope shall first unitt the two kingdoms of Scotland and England.' Sir William answered, 'Why, Madam? Shall he succeed before your Majestie and his father?' 'Because (sayes she) his father has broken to me.' The King was by and heard all. Sayes he, 'Sweet Madam, is this your promeis that you made to forgive and forgett all?' The queen answered, 'I have forgiven all, but will never forgett.' "

Lord Herries *Historie of the Regne of Marie, Queen of Scots.*

Charles I crowned King of Scotland at Holyroodhouse eight years after his accession, 1633.

20th

St Fillan, designated 'The Leper', an Irish saint who built his church on Loch Earn, 6th century.

22nd

Battle of Bothwell Brig, defeat of the Covenanters under Balfour of Burleigh and Hackston of Rathillet by the Royal Troops under the Duke of Monmouth, 1679.

"We intreated them to stand to the declaration, to let us go on against our enemy, and to let all debates alone till a free parliament and a general assembly. They told us we were for an indulgence, and they would sheathe their swords as soon in them who owned it as they would do in many of the malignants. . . We were not at this day past 4000 foot and 2000 horse; if we had agreed we would have been the triple, but when they came the one day they went away the next. The Lord took both courage and wisdom from us."

From the account by James Ure of Shargorton.

Declaration of the Covenanters against Charles II, 1680.

"Although we be for government and governors, such as the word of God and our covenant allows, yet we for ourselves and all that will adhere to us, as the representatives of the true presbyterian Kirk and covenanted nation of Scotland, considering the great hazard of lying under such a sin any longer, do by these presents disown Charles Stuart, that has been reigning (or rather tyrannising, as we may say) on the throne of Britain these years bygone, as having any right, title to, or interest in the said croun of Scotland, by his perjury and breach of covenant both to God and his Kirk, and usurpation of His croun and royal prerogatives therein."

Given at Sanquhar, June 22nd 1680.

23rd

Midsummer Een (St John's Eve), formerly celebrated by bonfires and torchlight processions to secure growing crops against the evil eye, the gathering of fern-seed and St John's wort as a charm against witches, Masonic processions, etc.

Combat between Bruce and Henry de Bohun before Bannockburn, 1314.

"Just as they met, Bruce shunn'd the spear.
Onward the baffled warrior bore
His course—but soon his course was o'er!
High in his stirrups stood the King,
And gave his battle-axe the swing.
Right on De Boune, the whiles he pass'd,
Fell that stern dint—the first—the last!"

Sir Walter Scott *The Lord of the Isles* canto vi.

Paul Crawar, from Bohemia, the second heretic to be burned in Scotland, died at St Andrews, 1433. James Resby, an English Wycliffite, was burned at Perth in 1407.

"Nocht lang efter was tane in Sanct Androis ane man of Beum namit Paule Craw, precheand new and vane superstitionis to the pepyl, specially aganis the sacarament of the alter, veneration of sanctis, and confession to be maid to Priestis. At last he was brocht afore the Theologis, and al his opinionis condampnit. And because he perseverit obstinatly to the end of his pley, he was condampnit and brint. He confessit afore his death that he was send out of Beum to preiche to Scottis the heresyis of Hus and Wiccleif".

Bellenden's *Boece* xvii. 6.

24th

St John the Baptist's Day, Midsummer Day.

Battle of Bannockburn, 1314.

"Scots wha hae wi' Wallace bled,
Scots wham Bruce has aften led,
Welcome to your gory bed,
Or to victorie!

Wha for Scotland's king and law
Freedom's sword will strongly draw,
Freeman stand or freeman fa,
Let him follow me!

Lay the proud usurpers low!
Tyrants fall in every foe,
Liberty's in every blow;
Let us do or die!

From Burns *Bruce's address to his army at Bannockburn.*

The Honours of Scotland, the Crown, Sword of State, and Sceptre of the Scottish Kings, carried in procession before the Queen on her first state visit to Scotland after her accession, 1953, the first occasion that the regalia had been borne in public since the visit of George IV to Edinburgh in 1822.

25th

St Moluag, "the pure and brilliant, the gracious and decorous, the sun of Lismore in Alba", 6th century.

26th

Formation of the Company which undertook the Darien Scheme and came to ruin five years later through English obstruction, Spanish hostility, and Scottish mismanagement, 1695.

"His Majesty understanding that several persons as well Forreigners as Natives of this kingdom are willing to engage themselves with great Soumes of Money in an American, Affrican, and Indian Trade, to be exercised in and from this Kingdom. . . to be one body incorporat, and a free incorporation, with perpetual succession, by the name of the Company of Scotland tradeing to Affrica and the Indies".

Acts of Parliament Scotland William III I. c. 10.

28th

Forth and Clyde Canal opened, 1790.

29th

The Yowes' Tremmle, a cold spell of about a week's duration occurring about now after the sheep shearing.

> "Ae weet forenicht i' the yow-trummle
> I saw yon antrin thing,
> A watergaw wi' its chitterin' licht
> Ayont the onding;
> An' I thocht o' the last wild look ye gied
> Afore ye deed!"
> Hugh MacDiarmid *The Watergaw.*

30th

Execution of the Earl of Argyll in Edinburgh, 1685.

"We parted sudenly but I hope shall meete hapily in heaven. I pray God bless you and if you seeke him he will be found of you".

From his last letter to his son.

Close season for the killing of stags ends.

JULY

Fallow ground as soon as the crop comes off. Ply, nail, prune, and dress your wall-trees. Pull up suckers and weeds. How and water where needful. Inoculate fruit-trees, shrubs, rare greens, and flower-trees; increase the same by laying. Clip your hedges after rain.

Sow turneep, radish, lettice, onion, coleflower, cabbage, and coleworts in the full moon. Near the end sow spinage, etc.

You may plant strawberries, violets. Lay July-flowers. Slip and set hypaticas, bearsears, helibors, etc. Take up bulbous and tuberous ones that are dry in their stalks (if you mind to change their places) and keep till September, but some should be set immediately.

Supply voids with potted annualls. Lay grass and gravell. Make cherrie and rasberrie wine, etc.

Prevent the bees' later swarms. Kill drons, wasps, etc.

John Reid *The Scots Gard'ner* (1683).

Third Tuesday (Old Style). Lilias Day at Kilbarchan.

16th or thereby. St Ronan's Games at Innerleithen.

"Folk had a jest that St Ronan dookit the Deevil in the Waal, which garr'd it taste aye since of brimstone."
Scott *St Ronan's Well* xv.

Third Week. Leith Races, transferred since 1816 to Musselburgh.

"Quod she, 'I ferly unco sair,
    That ye sud musand gae,
Ye wha hae sung o' Hallow-Fair,
    Her winter's pranks and play:
Whan on Leith Sands the racers rare,
    Wi' Jocky louns are met,
Their orro pennies there to ware,
    And drown themsel's in debt
        Fu' deep that day."
Robert Fergusson, *Leith Races*.

1st

St Serf (Servanus, Sair), of Culross and Lochleven, "the Apostle of Fife", tutor of St. Mungo (Kentigern), *c.* 700.

Seal of Cause granted by Edinburgh Town Council to the Incorporation of Barbers and Surgeons to practise their craft, 1505. This body is now the Royal College of Surgeons, Edinburgh.

Charter granted to Sir Alexander Fraser of Philorth to found a university at Fraserburgh, 1592.
> "To edifie and big up collegis, nocht onlie till the great decoirement of the cuntrey, bot also to the advancement of the loist and tint youthe in bringing tham up in leirning and vertew."
>> Act of Parliament 16 Dec. 1597 endowing the college.

North of Scotland Bank founded by Alexander Anderson and others in Aberdeen, 1836.

The Union Bank of Scotland, being an amalgamation over the years of the Ship Bank of Colin Dunlop and Houston, Coutts and Co., Forbes, Hunter and Co., Thistle Bank, Glasgow Union Bank, opens in Glasgow, 1843.

2nd

Treaty of Perth between Norway and Scotland, 1266.
> "That the same Lord Magnus, King of Norway, granted resigned and quit-claimed for himself and his heirs for ever, Man with the rest of the Sudreys and all other islands on the west and south of the Great Haf, with all rights which he and his progenitors had of old therein, the said islands to be held had and possessed by the said Lord Alexander III, King of Scots, and his heirs, . . . excepting the islands of Orkney and Zetland, which the said King of Norway has reserved specially to his dominion."
>> From the Latin of the Treaty.

3rd

James Crichton of Eliock, "the Admirable Crichton", graduate of St Andrews University, tutor of King James VI, soldier and scholar, killed in a brawl in Mantua, 1582.

"The Scotsman, James Crichton, is a youth who on the 19th of August last completed his 20th year. He is master of ten languages, Latin and Italian in perfection, and Greek so as to compose epigrams in that tongue, Hebrew, Chaldaic, Spanish, French, Flemish, English, and Scots, and he also understands the German. He is most skilled in philosophy, theology, mathematics, and astrology. . . He possesses a most thorough knowledge of the Cabala. His memory is so astonishing that he knows not what it is to forget. In his person he is extremely beautiful: his address is that of a finished gentleman. A soldier at all points, he has attained to great excellence in leaping and dancing and to a remarkable skill in the use of every sort of arms. He is a remarkable horseman and an admirable jouster."

> From a handbill by Domenico and Giovanni Battista Guerra, Venice, 1580.

5th

The Scottish Parliament establishes a General Post Office, 1695.

"Our Sovereign Lord, Considering that for the maintenance of mutual Correspondence several publick Post Offices have been heretofore erected . . . and that the well-ordering thereof is a matter of general concern and of great advantage, as well for the Conveniences of Trade and Commerce, as otherwayes, . . . statutes and ordains and appoynts a General Post Office to be keeped within the City of Edinburgh from whence all Letters and Packquets whatsoever may be with speed and expedition sent into any part of the Kingdom or any other of his Majesties Dominions or into any Kingdom or Contrey beyond Seas. . ."

> Acts of Parliament Scotland William III c. 31.

John Armstrong of Gilnockie, a border reiver, and 50 of his men, hanged for blackmail by James V at Carlanrig, 1530.

> "To seek het water beneath cauld ice,
>   Surely it is a great folie,
> I hae askit grace at a graceless face,
>   But there is nane for my men and me.
>
> But had I kenned, ere I cam frae hame,
>   How thou unkind wad been to me
> I wad hae keepit the border side,
>   In spite o' aa thy force and thee."
>   From the ballad of *Johnnie Armstrong*.

British Linen Bank chartered, 1746.
"His Majesty having been most graciously pleased at the Desire of sundry of the Nobility, Gentry, and Merchants of Great Britain, to grant them his Royal Charter incorporating them into a Body Politick for the more effectually promoting the Linen Manufactures of the Kingdom by the name and stile of the British Linen Company."
Advertisement of the first meeting, 11 August.

6th

Institute of Bankers in Scotland formed, 1875.
"This was the first such body in the world. . . . The apprenticeship system was soon augmented by the provision, by the Institute, of systematic teaching of the elements and evolution of banking and banking law."
S.G. Checkland, *Scottish Banking* 493.

7th

Death of King Edward I of England on his last punitive expedition to Scotland at Burgh-on-Sands near Carlisle, 1307.
"Edwardus Primus Scotorum Malleus hic est."
The epitaph in Westminster Abbey to "the hammer of the Scots."

The Raid of the Reidswire, one of the last skirmishes between
Scottish and English borderers, 1575.

> "Then raise the slogan with ane shout—
> 'Fy Tindaill to it! Jedbrugh's here!' "
>
> From the ballad in the Bannatyne MS.

8th

Abdication of King John Balliol at Montrose, 1296.

> "This Johne the Balliol spulyeit he Edward
> Off all his robis or ryalte,
> And tuke out the pelloure of his tabart,
> Tume Tabart thai callit him eftirwart;
> And all uthire insignyis
> That fell to king on ony wis
> As croune and cepture, suerd and ring,
> Fra this Johne, that he maid king,
> He tuke halely fra him thare,
> And maid him of the kinrik baire."
>
> Wyntoun *Chronicle* VIII xii.

Death of Sir Henry Raeburn, Scotland's foremost portrait painter
and King's Limner, 1822.

9th

Queen's Park Football Club formed, the first senior club in
Scotland, 1867.

10th

The first Bible printed in Scotland, 1579.

> Permission was given by the General Assembly in 1575 to
> "Alexander Arbuthnot, merchant burges of Edinburgh, and
> Thomas Bassanden, printer and burges of the said burgh" to
> print and publish a Bible in English at £4-13-4d Scots per
> copy. Bassandyne printed the New Testament in 1576, and after
> his death Arbuthnot completed the work in 1579, "all and haill

ane buke callit the Inglis bybill imprented of befoir at Geneva."

11th

St Drostan, evangelist of Buchan, founder of the Celtic abbey of Deer, 6th century.

Birth of Robert Bruce, later King of Scots, 1274.

12th

St Donald, a holy man of Glen Ogilvy in Angus, father of the Nine Maidens (see 18 July), c.716.

Rev. John Jamieson, D.D., minister of the Secession Church, compiler of "The Dictionary of the Scottish Language", died in Edinburgh, 1838.

13th

Alexander III crowned at Scone, 1249.

"It came to pass that . . . when this same earl, Walter Comyn, and all the clergy, and the Lord Malcolm, Earl of Fife, and the lord Malise, Earl of Strathearn, and a great many other nobles, led Alexander up to the cross which stands in the graveyard at the east end of the church. There they set him on the royal chair, which was decked with silken clothes inwoven with gold, and the bishop of St Andrews consecrated him king. So the king sat down upon the royal throne—that is, the stone— while the nobles on bended knee strewed their garments under his feet before the stone. . . But lo! when all was over, a highland Scot fell on his knees before the throne and hailed the king in his mother tongue, saying in Scottish, 'Benach de Re Albanne Alexander, MacAlexander, MacUilleam, Mac-Henri, MacDavid,' and so on unto the end of the pedigree of the kings of Scots."

From the Latin of Fordun *Annals of Scotland* xlviii.

Death of Henry Benedict Stewart, Cardinal, Bishop of Ostia, Dean of the Sacred College, the last of the royal house of Stewart, at Frascati, 1807.

"We wish here to renew and to express (as on the occasion of the death of Our Serene Brother) that so far as concerns the transmission of Our rights of Succession to the Throne and Crown of England in favour of that prince to whom it descends by virtue of blood-relationship, We transmit these rights to him with the most express and solemn form. . .

Enrico R. Cardinale."
From his will, 15 July 1802.

15th

The Gaelic poet, Alasdair MacMhaighstir Alasdair, dismissed from his S.P.C.K. school at Ardnamurchan for desertion of his post, 1745. He had gone off to welcome Prince Charles.

"Iorcallach garbh an tùs cleithe, 'G eigheach—'suas orr"
Iorram a dhuisgeas an spéirid Anns na guailnean
Sparras a' bhirlinn le séitrich Troimh gach fuar-ghleann
A' sgoltach nam bocthonn a' beucaidh Le saidh chruaidh chruim
Dh' iomaineas beanntanan béisteil Riomh da ghualainn.
'Hugan' le cuan, nullan gaireach 'Heig' air chnagan
Farum le bras-ghaoir na bhirlinn Ris na maidean.
(A stout man brawny at the fore-oar, crying 'Up with her'.
The rowing-song to rouse the vigour of the shoulders
To drive the galley snorting through each cold glen
Cleaving the swelling roaring waves with the hard curved stem
Driving the monstrous hills of water before the two bows;
'Hug', with the sea, the howling, the bellowing, 'Heig' on the thole-pins,
The clash with the sharp crack of the galley against the timbers)."
From his masterpiece *Birlinn Chlann-Raghnaill* (Clan Ranald's Galley).

17th

Establishment of the Bank of Scotland, 1695.
"Our soveraign lord, considering how usefull a Publick Bank

may be in this kingdom with the advice and consent of the Estates of Parliament allows a joynt stock amounting to the soume of twelve hundred thousand pounds money to be raised by the Company hereby established for the carrying on and manageing of a publick Bank . . . and all and every the persons subscribing and paying in to the said stock shall be and are hereby declared to be one Body Corporat and Politique by the name of 'The Governour and Company of the Bank of Scotland."

Acts of Parliament Scotland IX. 494.

Scottish Reform Bill becomes law, 1832, with celebrations in Edinburgh on August 11th.

"The Links were nearly filled—a fact which implies that from 30,000 to 40,000 must have been present, besides the 15,000 in procession. They passed an address to His Majesty, the House of Commons, and Earl Grey, and sang "God save the King", "Rule Britannia", and "Scots wha hae wi' Wallace bled". This part of the ceremony was sublime and effective, the last song particularly, which was joined in by thousands of voices all over the field, with the earnestness and devotion of a sacrament."

Lord Cockburn *Journal* I. 33.

18th

St Thenew, mother of St Kentigern, her name surviving as St Enoch in Glasgow, 6th century.

The feast of the Nine Maidens, daughters of St Donald of Glen Ogilvy (see July 12), associated with many holy wells (Nine [Maidens] Wells) throughout Scotland.

John Paul (John Paul Jones) born at Arbigland in Kirkcudbrightshire, 1747, Admiral of the United States Navy, died in Paris, 1792.

"In 1775 Paul Jones armed and embarked in the first American ship of war. In the Revolution he had twenty-three battles and solemn rencontres by sea, made seven descents in Britain and her colonies, took of her navy two ships of equal and two of superior force, many store ships and others, constrained her to fortify her ports, suffer the Irish volunteers, desist from the cruel burning in America and exchange as prisoners of war the American citizens taken on the ocean and cast into the prisons of England as traitors pirates and felons."

From an account of his life by himself.

19th

Battle of Halidon Hill at Berwick, crushing defeat of the Scots by Edward III of England and Edward Balliol, 1333.

"Bot many man thretes and spekes ful ill
That sumtyme war better to be stanestill;
The Skot in his wordes has wind for to spill,
For at the last Edward sall have al his will:
He had his will at Berwik, wele wurth the while;
Skottes broght him the kayes, bot get for thaire gile."

From Lawrence Minot, of Yorkshire.

20th

Act for establishing herring fishing in and around Scotland, 1705.

"Our Sovereign Lady and the Estates of Parliament taking to consideration the great and many advantages that may arise to this nation by encouraging the Salmond White and Herring fishing they being not only a natural and certain fund to advance the trade and increase the wealth thereof but also a true and ready way to breed seamen and set many poor and idle people to work."

Act of Parliament Scotland XI. 292.

21st

Burns died, 1796.

"Do for Heaven's sake send Mrs Armour here immediately. My wife is hourly expecting to be put to bed. Good God! what a situation for her to be in, poor girl, without a friend! I think and feel that my strength is so gone, that the disorder will prove fatal to me. Your son-in-law, R.B."

Burns's last letter, 19 July 1796.

22nd

Battle of Falkirk and defeat of the Scots under Sir William Wallace by King Edward I of England, 1298.

"So near the place called Fowkyrke, on the day of St Mary Magdalene, William Waleys set up a fence between the Scottish and English armies, fixing long stakes in the ground and joining them with cords to prevent the English charging his men. Then he posted the Scots infantry in the front line saying to them in their own language, 'Y have brought to the ryng. Hoppe yef ye kunne.'"

From the Latin of Thomas Walsingham *Historia Anglicana.*

Sir Archibald Johnston of Warriston, who drew up the National Covenant, member of the Westminster Assembly, Lord Advocate, Lord Clerk Register, executed in Edinburgh, 1663.

"Warriston was my own uncle. He was a man of great application, could seldom sleep above three hours in the twenty-four. He had studied the law carefully, and had a great quickness of thought, with an extra-ordinary memory. He went into very high notions of lengthened devotions, in which he continued many hours a day . . . He looked on the Covenant as the setting of Christ on His throne, and so was out of measure zealous in it. He had no regard to the raising himself or his family, though he had thirteen children; but presbytery was to him more than all the world."

Gilbert, Bishop Burnett, *History of my own Time.*

23rd

Laud's Prayer Book riot in St Giles, 1637.

"The Dean, Mr James Hanna, was mightilie upbraidit . . . One did cast a stool at him intending to have given him a ticket of remembrance; but jouking became his safeguard at that time... A good Christian woman betook herself to her Bible in a remote corner of the Church. A young man sitting behind her began to sound forth 'Amen!' At the hearing thereof, she quickly turned her about, and after she had warmed both his cheeks with the weight of her hands, she thus shot against him the thunderbolt of her zeal. 'False thief!' said she, 'is there no other part of the kirk to sing mass in, but thou must sing it at my lug?' "

From a pamphlet of the Covenanting period.

Prince Charles Edward lands in Eriskay, 1745.
"Two or three hours before landing, an eagle came hovering over the frigate. Before dinner the Duke of Athol had spied the eagle, and could not help remarking it to the Prince and his small retinue, which they looked upon with pleasure. His grace, turning to the Prince said, 'Sir, I hope this is an excellent omen, and promises good things to us. The king of birds is come to welcome your royal highness upon your arrival in Scotland' . . . When they landed in Eriskay they could not find a grain of meal or one inch of bread. But they catched some flounders, which they roasted upon the bare coals in a mean low hut they had gone into near the shore."
Bishop Forbes *The Lyon in Mourning*.

Death of Sir William Ramsay, born in Glasgow 1852, chemist, professor at Bristol and London, discoverer of the inert gases, helium, neon, radon, etc., Nobel prizeman 1904, died, 1916.

24th

Battle of Harlaw, 1411. Defeat of Donald MacDonald, Lord of the Isles, by the Crown forces under the Earl of Mar.
"As I cam in by Dunideer And doun by Netherha,
There were fifty thousand Hielandmen A' marchin to Harlaw,
    Wi a dree dree dradie drumtie dree.

If anyone did spier at you, Whare's the men ye had awa,
Ye may tell him plain and very plain, They're sleepin at
    Harlaw,
    Wi a dree dree dradie drumtie dree."
    From the traditional ballad.

Abdication of Mary Queen of Scots at Lochleven, 1567.
"Marie be the grace of God Quene of Scottis, forsamekle as be

lang irksum and tedious travell takin be us in the governament of this our Realme and liegis thairof, we ar sa vexit and weryit that our body spirite and sencis ar altogidder becum unhabill langer to travell in that rowme. And thairfore we have dimittit and renuncit the office of government of this our Realme and liegis thairof in favouris of our onlie maist deir sone, native Prince of this our Realme."

From the deed of abdication.

26th

Associated Friends of the People for Parliamentary Reform constituted in Edinburgh, 1792.

"Resolved that the object of this association be to attempt, by all constitutional means, the attainment, first, of an equal Representation of the People; and second, of a more limited Duration of Parliamentary Delegation."

From the notice in the *Caledonian Mercury* 28 July.

27th

Battle of Killiecrankie and death of John Graham of Claverhouse, Viscount of Dundee, 1689.

"Sir, It has pleased God to give your forces a great victory over the rebels, in which three-fourths of them have fallen under the weight of our swords . . . My wounds forbid me to enlarge to Your Majesty at this time, though they tell me they are not mortal. However, Sir, I beseech Your Majesty to believe, whether I live or die, I am entirely yours, Dundee.

Letter to James VII.

Scottish School of Design founded, 1760. It became the Royal Institution, now the Royal Scottish Academy in Edinburgh.

28th

The General Assembly approves the Westminster Shorter Cathechism, as "a Directory for catechising such as are of weaker capacity."

"Question 1. What is the chief end of man? Answer. Man's chief end is to glorify God and to enjoy him forever.
Question 2. What rule hath God given to direct us how we may glorify and enjoy him? Answer. The word of God, which is contained in the scriptures of the Old and New Testaments, is the only rule to direct us how we may glorify and enjoy him."

29th

St Olaf, King of Norway, killed, 1030. Several churches in Shetland and Orkney were dedicated to him.

Queen Mary married to her second husband, Henry Stewart, Lord Darnley, son of the Earl of Lennox, in Holyrood Chapel, 1565.
"Henry, duk of Albany, erll of rois, and Marie be the grace of God quen, Soverane of this realme, maryt in the Chappell."
From the Register of Marriages in the Canongate Parish.

James VI crowned at Stirling, 1567.
"The exhortatioun done, Adame bischope of Orknay anoyntit the said prince, and Johne erle of Athole put the croun on his head, according to the commission forsaid. The erle of Athole bure the croun, the erle of Mortoun the sceptour, and the erle of Glencairne the sword of honour, and the erle of Mar bure the king in his armes."
Diurnal of Occurrents.

30th

The beginning of the work-in at John Brown's Clydebank Shipbuilding yard, organised by James Reid, which led to the formation of Govan Shipbuilders and the take-over by Marathon Manufacturing with a liberal Government subsidy, 1971.

31st

Poems, chiefly in the Scottish Dialect published by John Wilson,

Kilmarnock, 1786. The first edition of Burns's poems.

"The following trifles are not the production of the Poet, who, with all the advantages of learned art, and perhaps amid the elegancies and idlenesses of upper life, looks down for a rural theme, with an eye to Theocrites or Virgil. To the Author of this, these and other celebrated names their countrymen are, in their original languages, 'a fountain shut up, and a book sealed'. Unacquainted with the necessary requisites for commencing Poet by rule, he sings the sentiments and manners he felt and saw in himself and his rustic compeers around him, in his and their native languages."

From the Preface.

AUGUST

Fallow bordures, beds, nurseries.

Yet inoculate. Pull up suckers and weeds. Clip hedges. Gather the seeds of most herbes and flowers. In the beginning sow cabbage (tho' I confess it's too late. See last month), spinage, lettice, corn-sallade, endive, etc.

Take up ripe onions, garleeks, and shallot. Unbind buds inoculated. Cut and string strawberries. Lay July-flowers. Sow columbines, holyhoks, larks-heels, candytuffs, popies, and such as can endure winter.

Take up your bulbs and plant as in the last. Sift the ground for tulips and gladiolus. Plunge in potted annualls in vacants. Keep down weeds by howing. Lay grass, beat, roll, and mow well. Make goosberrie and curran wine.

Towards the end take bees, take the lightest first; those that are near heaths may differ a little. Destroy wasps.

John Reid *The Scots Gard'ner* (1683).

1st

Lammas (Gaelic Lùnasdal), Autumn quarter-day in Scotland, festival of the new grain, when the cattle left the summer shielings, and many fairs were held throughout Scotland. There is still a Lammas Fair at St Andrews during the first week of the month.

Andrew Melville, Scottish Reformer, founder of the Presbyterian Church in Scotland, principal of Glasgow University and St Mary's College, St Andrews, born in 1545.

> "Howbeit the King used his authoritie in maist crabbit and colerik maner, yit Mr Andro bure him down and outtered the Commissioun as from the mightie God, calling the King bot 'God's sillie vassall', and taking him by the sleive sayss this in effect, 'Sir, I mon tell yow, ther is twa kings and twa kingdomes in Scotland. Thair is Chryst Jesus the King and his Kingdome the Kirk, whase subject King James the Saxt is, and of whase Kingdome nocht a king, nor a lord, nor a heid, bot a member."

Rev. James Melville Diary (1596).

George Lüdwig, great-grandson of King James VI, Duke of Brunswick-Lüneburg, succeeds to the throne of Great Britain as George I, of the House of Hanover, 1714.

> "Wha the deil hae we gotten for a king,
>   But a wee wee German lairdie?
> And when we gaed to bring him hame,
>   He was delvin in his yairdie,
> Sheughin kail and layin leeks,
>   But the hose and but the breeks,
> And up his beggar duds he cleeks,
>   This wee wee German lairdie."

From a popular Jacobite song of the time.

The wearing of tartan prohibited, 1747.

> "Be it further enacted that from and after 1st August 1747 no man or boy within that part of Great Britain called Scotland ... shall on any pretence whatever wear or put on the clothes commonly called Highland clothes, that is to say plaid, philebeg, or little kilt, trowse, shoulder belts, or any part whatsoever of what peculiarly belongs to the Highland garb; and that no tartan or plaid or stuff shall be used for great coats or for upper coats."

Acts 19 George II. 39.

The penalty for a first offence was six months imprisonment and for a second seven years transportation.

The separate representation of the Scottish peerage in terms of Article XXII of the Treaty of Union by sixteen of their members abolished, 1963.

The University of Dundee, formerly University College, Dundee, associated with the University of London, incorporated in the University of St Andrews, 1890, constituted as a separate university, 1967.

Wild duck shooting starts.

2nd

Death of Hamish MacCunn, born at Greenock, 1868, composer of music of a strongly Scottish cast, now best known for his overture *Land of the Mountain and the Flood*, in London, 1916.

Death of Alexander Graham Bell, born in 1847 in Edinburgh, inventor of the telephone, 1922.
> "The method of, and apparatus for, transmitting vocal or other sounds telegraphically, by causing electrical undulations similar in form to the vibrations of the air accompanying the said vocal or other sounds".
> U.S. Register of Patents, No. 174465, 7 March 1875.

3rd

King James II killed accidentally at the siege of Roxburgh Castle, 1460.

5th

Battle of Otterburn, 1388. James, Earl of Douglas, killed, and Henry Percy (Hotspur), son of the Earl of Northumberland, captured.
> "Ye lie, ye lie, ye liar loud, Sae loud I hear ye lie;
> For Percy had not men yestreen To dight my men and me.

> But I hae dreamed a dreary dream, Beyond the Isle of Skye;
> I saw a deid man win a fight, And I think that man was I.

This deed was done at Otterbourne About the breaking of the day;
Earl Douglas was buried at the bracken bush, And the Percy led captive away."
From the ballad of *Otterburn*.

The Gowrie Conspiracy, an attempt of Alexander, Lord Ruthven, and the Earl of Gowrie to seize King James at Gowrie House in Perth, 1600.

"Whereupon he, griping his Majestie by the wrest of the hand to have bound him, his Majestie releeved himselfe sodainely of his gripes. In this maner of wrestling, his Majestie perforce drew him to the window and under the which was passing by at the same time the Kings traine, and the Earl of Gowrie with them . . . and holding out the right side of his head and right elbow cryed that they were murthering him there . . . whose voice being instantly heard and knowne by the Duke of Lennox, the Earle of Marre and the rest of his Majesties traine, the saide Earle of Gowrie ever asking 'what it meant?' and never seeming to have seen his Majestie, or heard his voyce; they all rushed in at the gate together."
From the King's own narrative.

The Act of Security, which allowed the Estates of Scotland to chose another successor to Queen Anne than the one elected by the English Parliament if Scottish conditions were not met, approved, 1704. This precipitated an English demand for an Act of Union.

James Gibbs, architect, born in 1683 in Aberdeen, died in London, 1754. He designed St Martin's in the Fields Church, the Fellows' Building at King's College and the Senate House in Cambridge, the West Church of St Nicholas, Aberdeen, etc.

"All my printed books, books of architecture, books of prints and drawing-books of maps, and a pair of globes, to be placed in the Radcliffe Library in the University of Oxford of which I was architect."
From his will.

Death of Robert Mackay (Rob Donn), Gaelic poet of Sutherland, 1778.

6th

David Allan, Scottish genre painter, born in Alloa, 1744, well-known for his drawings of Edinburgh street scenes and rural life in the style of Hogarth, *The Gentle Shepherd, The Foulis Academy, The Penny Wedding*, etc. 1796.

8th

The Scottish Coronation Stone stolen from the Abbey of Scone by King Edward I, 1296.

"This chaire of merbell had sic fortoun and weird, that quhair it was fundin in ony land the samyn land sall pertene as natyve to Scottis, as ther versis schewis:

Nil fallat fatum, Scoti, quocunque locatum
Invenient lapidem, regnare tenentur ibidem
(The Scottish sall joyss and brouke the landis haill
Quhair thai fynd it, bot gif weirdis faill).

Throw quhilk happinit, that the said chair of merbill was eftir brocht owte of Spanye in Ireland; and furth of Ireland to Scotland. In the quhilk chair all kingis of Scotland war ay crownyt, quhill the tyme of King Robert Bruse. In quhilk tyme, besyde mony uther cruelties done be Edward Langschankis of Ingland, the said chair of merbill was takyn and brocht oute of Scoyn to Lundone, and eftir put in Westmonaster, quhair it remainis."

The legend as translated by John Bellenden from
Boece's *Scotorum Historiae* I. ii.

The procession of the Burry Man, originally to ensure a good harvest and fishing takes place at Queensferry about this time.

Marriage of James IV and Margaret Tudor, sister of Henry VIII, from which the Stewarts drew their claim to the throne of England, 1503.

"Than callit scho [Nature] all flouris that grew on feild,
Discirnyng all thair fassionis and effeiris,
Upon the awfull Thrissill scho beheld,

And saw him kepit with a busche of speiris;
Concedring him so able for the weiris,
A radius croun of rubeis scho him gaif,
And said, 'In feild go furth and fend the laif.'

Nor hald non udir flour in sic denty
As the fresche Ros of cullour reid and quhyt,
For gife thow dois, hurt is thyne honesty,
Conciddering that no flour is so perfyt,
So full of vertew, plesans, and delyt,
So full of blisfull angellik bewty,
Imperiall birth, honour and dignite."

> Dunbar *The Thrissill and the Rois,* written for the occasion.

9th

Thomas Telford, civil engineer, road, canal, harbour, and bridge builder, born in Dumfriesshire, 1757.

"In the year 1782 after having acquired the rudiments of my profession I considered that my native country afforded few opportunities of exercising it to any extent, and therefore judged it advisable (like many of my countrymen) to proceed southward, where industry might find more employment and be better rewarded."

> From his Autobiography.

10th

Education (Scotland) Act, providing for a state elementary education for all children, passed, 1872, amending and extending the previous provisions of the law of Scotland on education in the acts of 1696, 1793, 1839 and 1861.

11th

St Blane of Bute, the Lennox and Dunblane, died, c. 590.

12th

Shooting of grouse, ptarmigan and snipe begins.

14th

King Duncan I killed by Macbeth in battle at Bothnagowan near Elgin, 1040.

> "Duncan is in his grave;
> After life's fitful fever he sleeps well;
> Treason has done his worst: nor steel, nor poison,
> Malice domestic, foreign levy, nothing,
> Can touch him further."
> > Shakespeare *Macbeth* III. ii.

Mary, Queen of Scots, sets sail from Calais for Scotland, 1561.

> "Adieu, plaisant pays de France,
> O, ma patrie, la plus chérie,
> Qui as nourri ma jeune enfance,
> Adieu, France! Adieu mes beaux jours!
> La nef qui disjoint mes amours
> Ne cy de moi que la moitié;
> Une part te reste; elle est tienne,
> Je la fie à ton amitié,
> Pour que de l'autre il te souvienne."
> > Lines attributed to the Queen on the occasion by Meusnier de Querlon (*c.* 1760).

The University of Strathclyde constituted 1964. Formerly the Royal College of Science and Technology, created by the bequest by John Anderson in 1796 of the Technical Institution he had founded in Glasgow.

15th

Macbeth killed in battle at Lumphanan with Malcolm, son of King Duncan, 1057.

> " 'That man is noucht born of wiff
> Off power to reff me my lif.'
> The knycht said: 'I was nevir born,
> Bot of my modyr wayme was schorn.
> Now sal this tresson here tak ende,

And til thi fadyr I sal the sende.'
Thus Makbeth slew thai than
In to the wode of Lunfannan."
            Wyntoun *Chronicle* VI. xviii.

William Dunbar, author of *The Golden Targe, The Twa Marriet Wemen and the Wedo, The Lament for the Makaris,* etc., etc., appointed court poet, 1500.

"Lettre maid to Maister Williame Dunbar of the gift of ten lib. of pensioune to be pait to him of our Soverane Lordis cofferis be the Thesaurare for al the dais of his life or quhil he be promovit be oure Soverane Lord to a benefice of xl lib. or abone."
            From the Register of the Privy Seal.

Dunbar's answer:

"Welcum, my benefice and my rent,
And all the lyflett to me lent;
Welcum, my pensioun most preclair;
Welcum, my awin Lord Thesaurair!

Welcum, als heartlie as I can,
My awin dear maíster to your man,
And to your servant singulair;
Welcum, my awin Lord Thesaurair!"

Sir Walter Scott born in Edinburgh, 1771.

"Every Scottishman has a pedigree. It is a national prerogative, as unalienable as his pride and his poverty. My birth was neither distinguished nor sordid. According to the prejudices of my country, it was esteemed gentle, as I was connected, though remotely, with ancient families both by my father's and mother's side."
            From his *Autobiography.*

16th

Carolina Oliphant, poet, born at the old House of Gask in Perthshire, 1766.

"Oh, the auld laird, the auld laird, Sae canty, kind and crouse,

How mony did he welcome to His ain wee dear auld house!
And the leddy too, sae genty, There sheltered Scotland's heir,
And clipt a lock wi' her ain hand Frae his lang yellow hair."
    From her song *The Auld House.*

17th

The see of St Andrews made an Archbishopric by bull of Pope Sixtus
IV, 1472.

The Confession of the Faith and Doctrine, believed and professed by
the Protestants of Scotland, approved by the Estates of Parliament
and establishing the Reformation, 1560.
    "If any man will note in this our confession any article or
    sentence repugning to God's holy word, that it would please
    him of his gentleness, and for Christian charity's sake,
    admonish us of the same in writing."
        From the Preface.

The Cameron Highlanders commissioned by Letter of Service to
Alan Cameron of Erracht, 1793.
    "Having been favoured with the honour of embodying a
    Highland Regiment for His Majesty's service where could I go
    but to my native Lochaber? And with that desire I have
    decided on appealing to their forgiveness of bygone events and
    their loyalty to the Sovereign in his present exigencies."
        From a letter of Alan Cameron to his brother Ewen.

First Edinburgh International Festival of Music and the Arts opened,
1947.
    "The Edinburgh International Festival of Music and Drama
    was first discussed over a lunch table in a restaurant in
    Hanover Square, London, towards the end of 1944. Rudolf
    Bing was anxious to consider and investigate the possibility of
    staging such a Festival somewhere in the United Kingdom in
    the summer of 1946. . . Greatly daring, but not without
    confidence, I recommended Edinburgh as the centre and
    promised to make preliminary investigations."
        H. Harvey Wood in *The Scotsman.*

18th

St Inan, 9th century Ayrshire evangelist, with churches at Irvine and Beith, where a local holiday on this day is called Tenants (St Inan's) Day.

The Tay Road Bridge opened by Queen Elizabeth, the Queen Mother, in 1966. The longest road bridge in the United Kingdom, 7356 feet long on double piers. Cost £6,500,000.

19th

Queen Mary landed at Leith from France, 1561.
> "At the sound of the cannonis whiche the galayis schot, the multitude being advertissed, happie was he and sche that first myght have the presence of the Quene. The Protestantis war not the slowest, and thairintill thai war not to be blamed. Becaus the Palace of Halyrudhous was not throughlie put in ordour, sche remaned in Leyth till towardis the evenyng and then repaired thither."
> John Knox *History* II. 269.

Prince Charles's standard unfurled at Glenfinnan to start the Jacobite Rising, 1745.
> "On the 19th they proceeded to Glenfinnan at the head of the loch in Clanranald's country, and there set up his standard on which there was no motto at all, and was immediately joined by Lochiel, Keppoch, and others, with 1400 men in all."
> *Lyon in Mourning* I. 292.

James Watt died, 1819.
> "I had gone to take a walk on a fine Sabbath afternoon (on Glasgow Green in May 1765). I was thinking upon the engine and had gone as far as the herd's house, when the idea came into my mind that as steam was an elastic body, it would rush into a vacuum, and if a communication were made between the cylinder and an exhausted vessel, it would rush into it and might be condensed without cooling the cylinder."
> From his own account to Robert Hart, 1814.

20th

Black grouse shooting starts.

St Ronald, Earl of Orkney, killed, 1158. Canonised 1192.
"Earl Rognvald died on the fifth day after the Feast of the Assumption. Earl Harald and his men sailed in great style from Thurso to Orkney with the body, and buried it in St Magnus Cathedral where Earl Rognvald rested until God made manifest the worthiness of the Earl with a number of wondrous miracles."
Orkneyinga Saga § 104.

21st

William Murdoch, inventor of gas-lighting, assistant to James Watt, born at Auchinleck, 1754.

22nd

Battle of the Standard, and total defeat of the Scots under David I by the English near Northallerton, 1138.
"At the same time the army of the Scots cried out the war-cry of their fathers, and the shout rose even to the skies, Albanaich, Albanaich!"
Henry of Huntingdon *Historia Anglorum* 263.

Devorgilla, Countess of Galloway, founded Balliol College, Oxford, 1282.
"Devorgilla of Galloway, Lady of Balliol, to our beloved in Christ, brother Hugh of Hertilpoll and Master William of Menyl, health in the Lord perpetual, desiring with maternal affection to provide for the profit of our sons and scholars sojourning at Oxford . . . "
From the original Latin Charter.

Execution of Sir William Wallace in London, 1305.
"This grace he ast at Lord Clyfford that knycht,
To lat him haiff his Psaltyr buk in sycht,

He gert a preyst it oppyn befor him hauld,
Quhill thai till him had done all at thai wald;
Stedfast he red, for ocht thai did him thar."
            Blind Harry *Wallace* XI.

"The story of Wallace poured a Scottish prejudice into my
veins, which will boil along there till the flood-gates of life
shut in eternal rest."
            Burns *Letter to Dr Moore* 2 Aug. 1787.

The Statutes of Icolmkill agreed upon by the chieftains of the Isles
before Bishop Andrew Knox of the Isles at Iona, 1609.
   "1.   The ministeris within the parrochynis of the saidis Illandis
salbe reverentlie obeyit . . .
   5.   No persone or personis indwellairis within the boundis of
the saidis haill Iles bring in to sell for money ather wyne or
acquavitae under the pane of tinsale of the samyn.
   6.   Every gentilman or yeaman sall put at leist their eldest
sone, or having no childrene maill thair eldest dochter, to the
scuillis on the Lawland quhill they may be found able
sufficientlie to speik, reid, and wryte Inglische . . . "
            Register of the Privy Council (1610) 69-70.

24th

"Act anent the keiping of the Sabaoth day," 1568.

25th

St Ebba, Abbess of Coldingham, and of St Abb's Head, died, 683.

Sir James Douglas died in battle over Bruce's heart at Tebas in
Spain, 1330.
            "Amang the hethin men the hert hardely he slang,
            Said, 'Wend on as thou was wont
            Throw the batell in bront
            Ay formast in the front
            Thy fayis amang."
            R. Holland *Buke of the Howlat* xxxviii.

Death of David Hume, philosopher and historian, 1776.

"A man of mild dispositions, of command of temper, of an open, social and cheerful humour, capable of attachment but little susceptible of enmity, and of great moderation in all my passions. Even my love of literary fame, my ruling passion, never soured my humour notwithstanding my frequent disappointments. My company was not unacceptable to the young and careless, as well as to the studious and literary: and as I took particular pleasure in the company of modest women, I had no reason to be displeased with the reception I met with from them . . . though I wantonly exposed myself to the rage of both civil and religious factions, they seemed to be disarmed in my behalf of their wonted fury; not but that the zealots, we may well suppose, wou'd have been glad to invent and propagate any story to my disadvantage, but they coud never find any which, they thought, woud wear the face of probability."

From his memoir *My Own Life.*

Scottish Parliamentary Labour Party inaugurated, with R.B. Cunninghame Graham as President and James Keir Hardie as secretary, in Glasgow, 1888.

"Resolved that its object be to educate the people politically, and to secure the return to Parliament and all local bodies of members pledged to its programme."

27th

St Maol Rubha of Applecross, 640-722, with many dedications in North and West Scotland. Loch Maree in Rossshire and Summereve's Fair at Keith in Banffshire bear his name. He was a descendant of Niall of the Nine Hostages.

The General Assembly approves the Westminster Confession of Faith, 1647.

28th

Bull of Pope Benedict XIII ratifying the founding of St Andrews University, 1413.

"That the said University may be rich in the honour of its students we take your foresaid University and you all present and to come, whom we honour with the privilege of our peculiar love, under the perpetual protection of ourselves and our successors, in virtue of the regality of our church of St Andrews."

From the Latin of the Bull.

29th

Battle of Tranent, 1797. A demonstration against conscription under the Militia Act was broken up by the Cinque Ports Dragoons and the East Lothian Yeomanry with the deaths of twelve participants.

"We declare that we unanimously disapprove of the late Act of Parliament for raising Six Thousand Militiamen in Scotland.

We will assist each other in endeavouring to repeal the said Act.

We are peaceably disposed, and should you in endeavouring to execute the said Act urge us to adopt coercive measures we must look upon you to be the aggressors and as responsible to the nation for all the consequences that may follow."

From the demonstrators' declaration.

The evacuation of the population from St Kilda on economic grounds, 1930.

30th

St Fiacre, probably a Scottish saint, who laboured in France, died, 670.

He is the patron saint of gardeners and has a church dedication at St Fittick's, Nigg, Aberdeen. Hackney cabs got their French name *fiacre* from being first hired in Paris from an establishment at the Hôtel de St Fiacre.

Trial of Thomas Muir, advocate, of Huntershill, for sedition, 1793. He was sentenced to 14 years' transportation.

"Mr Muir might have known that no attention could be paid to such a rabble. What right had they to representation? He could have told them that the parliament would never listen to their petition. How could they think of it? A government in every country should be just like a corporation; and in this country it is made up of the landed interest, which alone has a right to be represented; as for the rabble who have nothing but personal property, what hold has the nation of them? What security for the payment of their taxes? They may pack up all their property on their backs and leave the country in the twinkling of an eye, but landed property cannot be removed."

From Lord Justice-Clerk Braxfield's address to the jury.

SEPTEMBER

The third sesone that is callit autumpne, that we call hervist, the quhilk begynnis quhen the sonne enteris in a signe callit the Balance, that begynnis the xxiii day of September and lestis quhill the xxiii day of the moneth of December. And in that begynnyng of tyme the nycht and the day is ylike lang, and ay growis the nycht and schortis the day to the end of that terme. And the ayre worthis cald, and the wynde sourar and cummys commounly out of the south, and the tyme changis and wateris wanis, and wellis stryndis lessis, and all growth gais bakwart, and all greness away gais, and herbis and flouris and fuellis rottis and drawis till a fadand hewe, and the erde tynis his beautee, and the treis thair clething, and the foulis thair singing and sekis till hate landis and warmare regionis, and serpentis enteris in thair cavernis, the emotis gaderis to thair provisionis for aganis the wynteris to thair nestis, the quhilk tyme is comperit till ane alde wyfe gangand bakwart, in the quhilk tyme thare haboundis in men a thing callit colare nygre that drawis to melancoly.

From Gilbert Hay *Buke of the Governaunce of Princis* (1456).

Fallow, trench, and level ground. Prepare pits and bordures for trees. Gather ripe fruits. Plant furth cabbage. Remove bulbs and plant them. Refresh, traine, and house your tender greens. Refresh and trim pots and cases with July-flowers and other fine flowers and plants; carrying them to pits shelter and covert, giving them air. Towards the end gather saffron.

Make cyder and other wines.

Straiten the entrance to bee-hives, destroy wasps, etc. Also you may now remove bees.

John Reid *The Scots Gard'ner* (1683).

1st

St Giles (Aegidius), a Greek saint who evangelised in France, patron saint of Edinburgh and Elgin, died, 714.

Partridge and woodcock shooting begins.

3rd

The Scottish Covenanting army of Charles II, King of Scots, under Sir David Leslie, routed by the English Parliamentarians under Oliver Cromwell at Dunbar, 1650.

"Hodgson heard him say, 'They run! I profess they run!' And over St Abb's Head and the German Ocean, just then, bursts the first gleam of the level Sun upon us, 'and I heard Nol say, in the words of the Psalmist, 'Let God arise, let his enemies be scattered', or in Rous's metre,

Let God arise, and scattered Let all his enemies be;
And let all those that do him hate Before his presence flee!"

Carlyle, *Cromwell's Letters and Speeches* VI. Letter cxxxix.

James Francis Stewart proclaimed as King James VIII of Scotland by his son, Prince Charles Edward at Perth, 1745.

"We see a Nation always famous for Valour, and highly esteemed by the greatest of foreign Potentates, reduced to the Condition of a Province, under the specious pretence of an Union with a more powerful Neighbour. .

We do therefore by this our Royal Declaration, absolutely and effectually pardon and remit all Treasons, and other Crimes hitherto committed against our Royal Father or ourselves . . .

We further declare that we will, with all convenient speed, call a free Parliament . . .

We likewise promise, upon our Royal Word, to protect, secure and maintain all our Protestant Subjects in the free Exercise of their Religion, and in the full Enjoyment of all their Rights, Privileges, and Immunities and in the secure Possession of all Churches, Universities, Colleges, and Schools,

conform to the Laws of the Land . . .
> Given at Rome the 23rd day of December, 1743."

Weavers' riot against wages-cutting in Glasgow, 1787.
> "The misunderstanding that has subsisted for some time past betwixt the manufacturers of muslin and their workmen, terminated on Monday in a very melancholy manner . . . Stones and bricks were thrown at the magistrates and military, and several much hurt. Orders were then given to the soldiers to fire, when three persons were killed, three mortally wounded, and several slightly. The crowd then dispersed."
> *Scots Magazine,* Sept. 1787.

Forth Road Bridge opened, 1964.
> The largest suspension bridge in Europe, it is over a mile and a half long, including approach roads, and has a central span of 3,300 feet and side spans of 1,340 feet, two main towers each 512 feet high and a 24 feet dual carriageway with paths at the sides for cyclists and pedestrians. The bridge is 208 feet above the water at midstream, the total cost being about £20,000,000.

5th

Robert Fergusson, poet, born in the Canongate of Edinburgh, 1750.
> "At times when she may lowse her pack,
> I'll grant that she can find a knack
> To gar auld-warld wordies clack
> In hamespun rhyme,
> While ilk ane at his billy's back
> Keeps gude Scots time."
> From his *Epistle to Mr J.S.*

Death of John Home in 1808. Born at Leith, 1722, formerly minister at Athelstaneford, playwright, he was especially noted as author of the historical drama *Douglas,* first produced in Edinburgh, 1756, to the denunciations of the Edinburgh Presbytery, which led to Home's resignation from the ministry. He later became secretary to Lord Bute, the Prime Minister, and tutor to the Prince of Wales, and was the last Conservator or Consul for Scottish trade with the Netherlands at Veere.

"The opinion which the Christian Church has always entertained of stage plays and players as prejudicial to the interest of religion and morality is well known, and the fatal influence which they commonly have on the far greater part of mankind, particularly the younger sort, is too obvious to be called in question."

From the Presbytery's "Admonition", 5 Jan. 1757.

6th

The standard of the Old Pretender unfurled by the Earl of Mar at Braemar in the first Jacobite Rising, 1715.

The colour was blue, on one side the Scottish arms in gold, on the other the thistle, with the mottoes 'No Union' and 'Nemo me impune lacesset' and white pennants with the inscriptions 'For our wronged king and oppressed country' and 'For our lives and liberties'.

"The standard on the Braes o' Mar Is up and streaming rarely;
The gathering pipe on Lochnagar Is sounding lang and sairly.
The Hieland men frae hill and glen, In martial hue, wi' bonnets blue,
Wi' belted plaids and burnished blades, Are coming late and early."

From the song by Alexander Laing.

The Porteous Riot, 1736.

"Whereas it hath been represented unto us, that a great number of wicked, dissolute, and disorderly Persons did . . . assemble and conveen themselves together in the City of Edinburgh, and seize the Arms of the Guard of the said City ... and did likewise break open the Tolbooth or Prison of the said City, by setting Fire to the Gates thereof, and thereby set at large the several Prisoners therein confined for divers Crimes, and did thereout in a most cruel Manner, drag John Porteous, commonly called Captain John Porteous, there also confined under a Judgment and Sentence of Death, the Execution whereof had been by a Reprive granted by us respited, and did most barbariously and inhumanly murder the said John Porteous by hanging him up by the neck until he was dead . . ."

From the Proclamation by Queen Caroline for discovering the Murderers, 25 Sept. 1736.

Birth of William Livingston, Gaelic poet, in Islay, 1808. His verse is of a strongly nationalist cast.

"The inherited houses of those who have left us are cold cairns throughout the land. Gone are the Gaels and they shall not return. The cultivation has ceased; there is no more sowing and reaping. The stones of the melancholy larochs bear witness."

From his *Fios thun a' Bhaird.*

Andrew Hardie and John Baird, Glasgow weavers, hanged at Stirling for high treason, 1820. They were involved in the so-called 'Radical Rising' and the 'battle' of Bonnymuir, 5 April, precursors of the Reform Movement.

"(1)   Compassing and Imagining the death of the King;
(2)   Conspiring to levy War and to subvert the Constitution.
(3)   For endeavouring to seduce the Troops of the King from their allegiance.
(4)   For forcing divers subjects to discharge and turn off their Workmen.
(5)   For striking work and compelling and persuading others to do the same."

From the counts of the indictment against them.

Scottish Co-operative Wholesale Society begins business in Glasgow, 1868.

"That this conference, convinced of the advantage and necessity of a wholesale agency, and seeing that the North of England Co-operative Wholesale Society cannot extend a branch to Scotland, hereby appoint a committee to diffuse information, make the necessary arrangements for commencing a wholesale co-operative society in Glasgow, and in the meantime make use of the North of England Society for the supply of our wants as shall be deemed desirable."

Resolution of Conference of Scottish Societies, 8th June 1867.

9th

Battle of Flodden and the defeat and death of James IV and the flower of Scotland, 1513.

> "To town and tower, to down and dale,
> To tell red Flodden's dismal tale,
> And raise the universal wail.
> Tradition, legend, tune, and song.
> Shall many an age that wail prolong:
> Still from the sire the son shall hear
> Of the stern strife and carnage drear,
>   Of Flodden's fatal field,
> Where shivered was fair Scotland's spear,
>   And broken was her shield."
>
> Scott *Marmion* VI. xxxiv.

Christopher Murray Grieve ("Hugh MacDiarmid"), Scotland's foremost modern poet, born in Langholm 1892, died in Edinburgh, 1978.

> "Mars is braw in crammasy,
> Venus in a green silk goun,
> The auld mune shaks her gowden feathers,
> Their starry talk's a wheen o blethers,
> Nane for thee a thochtie sparin',
> Earth, thou bonnie broukit bairn!
> But greet, an' in your tears ye'll droun
> The haill clanjamfrie!"
>
> Hugh MacDiarmid *The Bonnie Broukit Bairn.*

10th

Robert Henryson admitted to Glasgow University as Licentiate in Arts and Bachelor of Law, 1462. Probably the poet Henryson, author of the *Moral Fabillis, The Testament of Creisseid,* etc.

> "Quha wait gif all that Chauceir wrait was trew?
> Nor I wait nocht gif this narratioun
> Be authoreist, of fenyeit of the new
> Be sum poeit, throw his inventioun,
> Maid to report the lamentatioun

And wofull end of this lustie Creisseid,
And quhat distres scho thoillit and quhat deid."
From his *Testament of Cresseid* x.

Battle of Pinkie, 1547.
"Sum sayis that the Scottismen was betraissit be sum of thair
awin, and uther sum sayis that it was thair awin pryde and
presumptousnes and arrogance and willfullnes that wald not
heire no gude ressonabill affaris of the Inglischmen nor be
content to have no peace with thame for no way, thairfor God
sieand thame so willfull heigh and proud that He punischt
thame by expectatioun of men. For He sent sic feir and
dreadour in thair hairtis that they fled and knew nocht
quhairfor."
Pitscottie *Croniclis* XXII. xvi.

11th

Battle of Stirling Bridge, 1297. Defeat of the English army under the
Earl of Surrey and the Treasurer of England, Cressingham, by the
Scottish Guardians, Wallace and Andrew de Moray.
"Having in time past struck others with terror by the spear of
his tongue, he [Cressingham] perished at last by the spears of
evil men. The Scots flaying him divided the skin amongst them
in small pieces, not as relics, but by way of contumely; for
indeed he was handsome and very stout, and was called not
treasurer but betrayer of the king, as they believed; for he had
led away many that day, but was himself led away, being light
and slippery, lofty, proud, and given to avarice."
From the Latin of the *Chronicle of Guisborough*.

The Privy Council recommends a licence to mine copper in
Midlothian, 1683.
"The many attempts for finding out and working of copper
mines within this kingdom having hitherto proved altogether
uneffectuall, . . . and there being a German here called
Joachim Gouel who is a skilfull man and hath been conversing
all his life in such things, he is content to begin so desirable a
work without any other encouragement than a gift of a

particular copper mine lying within the parish of Currie."
Register of the Privy Council VIII. 241.

Death of James Thomson, Born at Ednam in 1700, poet of *The Seasons* and various tragedies, died, 1748.

> "When Britain first at Heaven's command
> Arose from out the azure main,
> This was the charter of her land,
> And guardian angels sung the strain:
> Rule Britannia! Britannia rules the waves!
> Britons never shall be slaves."
> From his *Masque of Alfred.*

Mungo Park, doctor, African explorer, born near Selkirk, 1771.

Park made two unsuccessful journeys to find the source of the Niger, but was able to plot part of its course, and to describe the slave trade in the Sahara in his *Travels*, published in 1799. He was killed by native tribes in 1806.

13th

Battle of Philiphaugh and defeat of the Royalist troops under Montrose by the Covenanting army under Sir David Leslie, 1645.

> "On Philiphaugh a fray began, At Hairheadwood it ended;
> The Scots outoer the Graemes they ran, Sae merrily they bended."
> From the ballad on the battle in Scott's *Minstrelsy.*

14th

Ruid Day (in hairst), the day of the Exaltation of the Cross.
Cf. 3rd May.

15th

St Mirren, patron saint of Paisley, 6th century.

Edinburgh High School Riot, 1595.

> "This John MacMorrane being baillie for the tyme, the bairns
> of the said gramar schooll came to the tounes counsell

conforme to their yeirlie custome to seek the priviledge, quha
wes refusit; upon the quhilk ther wes ane number of schollaris
made ane mutinie and came in the night and took the schooll. .
The said baillie and officers tooke ane geast and ran at the
back dore . . . Ther came ane schollar callit William Sinclair
and with ane pistolet shott out at ane window, and shott the
said baillie throw the heid, sua that he diet."

From Robert Birrel *Diary*.

Death of Andrew Fletcher of Saltoun, soldier, essayist, improver,
Commissioner for Haddington in the Scottish Parliament, opponent
of the Union, 1716.

"Poor Salton who has appeared all along very much concerned
for the condition of his countrymen, died last week at London,
and since ever he got the accounts of these people [Jacobite
prisoners] being carried to England, never was well. The last
words he spoke were, 'My poor country!' He has left the
prisoners £200."

Letter from Sir Hugh Paterson to the Earl of Mar, 9
Oct.

16th

St Ninian, disciple of St Martin of Tours, founder of Candida Casa,
later Whithorn Abbey, evangelised southern Scotland, 4th-5th
century.

17th

Prince Charles enters Holyroodhouse, 1745.

"When Charles came to the Palace he dismounted and walked
along the piazza towards the apartment of the Duke of
Hamilton. When he was near the door, which stood open to
receive him, a gentleman stepped out of the crowd, drew his
sword and raising his arm aloft, walked upstairs before
Charles. The person who enlisted himself in this manner was
James Hepburn of Keith . . . He had been engaged when a
very young man in the rebellion of the year 1715, and
condemned the Union between England and Scotland as

injurious and humiliating to his country; saying (to use his own words) that the Union had made a Scotch gentleman of small fortune nobody, and that he would die a thousand times rather

than submit to it."
John Home *History of the Rebellion.*

19th

The Great North of Scotland Railway opened from Aberdeen to Huntly, 1854.

20th

Prince Charles Edward left Scotland for the last time, 1746.

"The Prince being now informed that the French ships were in Lochnanuagh waiting for him, set out immediately accompanied by Lochiel, Lochgarie, John Roy Stuart, etc., and going on board the Happy privateer of St Maloes, she immediately set sail the twentieth of September, and escaping all the Government's warships, and being in her way happily favoured by a fog, he arrived safely in France."
Lockhart Papers II. 562.

"Will ye no come back again, Will ye no come back again?
Better lo'ed ye canna be, Will ye no come back again?"
Lady Nairne *Will ye no come back again?*

21st

Battle of Prestonpans and defeat of the Hanoverian army under Sir John Cope by Prince Charles and the Jacobites, 1745.

"When Johnie Cope to Dunbar came,
They spiered at him 'Whaur's a' your men?'
'The deil confound me gin I ken,
For I left them a' in the mornin'.

'Now, Johnie, troth, ye arena blate
To come wi the news o your ain defeat,
And leave your men in sic a strait
Sae early in the mornin'."
From Adam Skirving
Hey, Johnie Cope, are ye waukin yet?

Death of Sir Walter Scott, 1832.

> "Scott is dead. He expired yesterday. I had been on a visit to Kirklands, and on coming home today I saw Abbotsford reposing beside its gentle Tweed, and amidst its fading woods, in the calm splendour of a sweet autumnal day. I was not aware till I reached Edinburgh that all that it then contained of him was his memory and his remains. Scotland never owed so much to one man."
>
> Lord Cockburn *Journal*.

23rd

St Adamnan of Iona, biographer of Columba, died, 704.

Commission to the Earl of Mar to raise a regiment to suppress the Covenanters, 1678, hence the nickname "Earl of Mar's Gray Breeks", later the Royal Scots Fusiliers and now, by amalgamation with the H.L.I., the Royal Highland Fusiliers since 1959.

25th

St Barr, 6th century Irish saint, bishop of Cork, from whom the island of Barra takes its name.

26th

James Keir Hardie, born at Holytown, 1836, coal-miner, labour activist, founder of the Scottish Labour Party, chairman of the I.L.P., M.P. for West Ham and Merthyr Tydfil, anti-war propagandist, died at Cumnock, 1915.

> "He made the British working-class politically conscious. But he was very far from being a typical working man. He was a lonely, isolated individual, who fitted in with difficulty into any mass organisation. His religious mysticism, his concern with spiritualism and with thought transference, his belief in a previous incarnation for humans and for beasts alike, his attachment to old folk myths, to the Druids, to oral tradition, to the sustaining force of mother earth—these were facets of the essential Hardie too."
>
> K.O. Morgan *Keir Hardie* 289.

27th

Scotland's first railway, Glasgow Townhead to Garnkirk, opened to passenger traffic, 1837.

28th

Clan fight on the North Inch at Perth, 1396.
> "A great part of the North of Scotland was disturbed by two wretched caterans and their followers—Scheabeg and his kinsmen, who are known as the Clan Kay, and Cristi Jonson with his kin, who are called the Clan Quhele. . . At length the noble and industrious Sir David of Lindsay of Crawford and Sir Thomas, Earl of Moray, brought the parties to this mutual agreement—that on a certain day they would appear before the King at Perth, and each party choosing thirty of their kindred, they would fight each other, armed only with swords and bows and arrows, and without doublets or other armour save poleaxes."
> From the Latin of W. Bower *Scotichronicon.*

George Buchanan, humanist, poet, historian of Scotland, tutor of James VI, reformer, died, 1582.
> "Mr Thomas, his cusing, schawes him of the hardness of that part of his Storie, that the king wald be offendit with it, and it might stey all the wark. 'Tell me, man,' sayes he, 'giff I have tauld the treuthe?' 'Yis,' sayes Mr Thomas, 'Sir, I think sa'. 'I will byd his fead, and all his kins, then, quoth he, 'Pray to God for me, and let Him direct all.' "
> Rev. James Melville *Diary*, 1581.

The Cunard-White Star *Queen Mary* launched at Clydebank, 1934.
> Then the world's largest liner. Built by John Brown and Sons, Ltd. Gross tonnage: 81,235 tons. Length: 975.2 feet. Breadth: 118.6 feet. Depth: 68.5 feet. Speed: 28 knots.

29th

Michaelmas. In the Highlands the day of the *struan* or richly flavoured oatcake.

"An Beannachadh Struain.
Gach min tha fo mo chleibh, Theid am measgadh le cheil
An ainm Mhic De Thug fas daibh.
Bainn is uibheann is im, Sochair mhaith ar cuid fhein.
Cha bhi gainne 'n ar tir, No 'n ar fardraich."
(The Blessing of the Struan. Each meal that is beneath my roof,
they will be mixed together in the name of the Son of God
who gave growth to them. Milk and eggs and butter, the good
produce of our own stock. There shall be no lack in our place
nor in our dwelling).

A. Carmichael *Carmina Gadelica* I. 215.

Charter to colonise Nova Scotia granted to Sir William Alexander of
Menstrie, 1621.

"Our pleasure is, that yow graunt unto the sayd Sir William,
his heires and assignes, or to anie other that will joyne with
him . . . a Signatour under our Great Seale of the sayde lands
lying between New England and Newfoundland, To be holden
of us from our Kingdome of Scotland as a part thereof."

Letter of King James to the Privy Council of Scotland,
5 Aug. 1621.

OCTOBER

Gather winter fruits. Trench and fallow grounds (mixing with proper soil) to ly over the winter. Prepare manures, mixing and laying in heaps bottom'd and covered with earth. Plant hawthorn hedges, and all trees that lose their leaves. Also lay their branches. Prune roses. Cut strawberries, artichocks, asparagus, covering their beds with manure and ashes. Earth up winter sallades, herbes and flowers a little. Plant cabbage, tulips, anemonies and other bulbs. Sow the seed of bairsears, cowslips, etc. Beat and roll gravel and grass. Finish your last weeding and mowing. Delve and manure such trees as require it. Drain excessive moisture wherever it be. Pickle and conserve fruits. Make perry and cyder.

    You may now safely remove bees.

        John Reid *The Scots Gard'ner* (1683).

The Bannatyne MS., the most extensive collection of early Scottish poetry extant, made by George Bannatyne, merchant of Edinburgh, while staying at Newtyle in Angus to escape the plague, 1568.

    "Heir endis this buik, writtin in tyme of pest,
    Quhen we fra labor was compeld to rest
    Into the thre last monethis of this yeir,
    From oure Redemaris birth, to knaw it heir,
    Ane thousand is, fyve hundreth, threscoir aucht."
        From the Envoi of the Collection.

2nd

The Battle of Largs, and defeat of the Norsemen, leading to the cession of the Hebrides and Man to Scotland, 1263.

"Hakon, the King of Norway, with a large number of ships came west over the sea to attack the King of Scotland, but in fact as Hakon himself admitted he was repulsed not by human force but by divine power which wrecked his ships and sent a plague on his army; and besides through the serving-men of the country attacked and routed those who had gathered for battle on the third day after Michaelmas. So they were forced to return to their ships with their dead and wounded; and so to go back to their land with less honour than when they set out."

From the Latin of the *Chronicle of Melrose*, 190.

Reunion of the Church of Scotland and the United Free Church of Scotland as the Church of Scotland, 1929.

"Behold, how good a thing it is, And how becoming well Together such as brethern are In unity to dwell."
Psalm cxxxiii. 1.

3rd

Battle of Glenlivat and the defeat of the Royal troops under the Earl of Argyll by Catholic lords under the Earl of Huntly, 1594.

From this incident arose the proverb: Is fad an éubh o Loch Obha, 's cobhair o chlann O'Duibhne (It's a far cry from Loch Awe and help from Clan O'Duibhne [the Campbells and their territory]).

7th

St Syth, the patron saint of those who have lost something, commemorated in Kilsyth.

"Thai rin, quhen thai haif jowellis tinte,
To seik Sanct Syth or evir thai stynte."
                    Sir David Lindsay *The Monarchie* 2369.

Thomas Reid, born at Strachan 1710, professor of moral philosophy
at Aberdeen and Glasgow, countered the scepticism of Hume with
the contention that much of our knowledge is intuitive and *a priori*,
the philosophy of "Common Sense", died at Glasgow, 1796.

Close season for trout fishing begins.

8th

St Triduana, who is said in legend to have blinded herself to escape
the attentions of an unwanted suitor and is buried at Restalrig in
Edinburgh.

9th

Act "in favour of Universities Schools and Hospitalls", 1696. "For
the more easy and speedy ingathering of their Stipend."

10th

Hugh Miller, self-taught geologist, essayist, journalist, author of
*Footprints of the Creator, The Old Red Sandstone, The Testimony of the
Rocks*, etc., born in Cromarty, 1802.
    "Life itself is a school, and Nature always a fresh study—and
    the man who keeps his eyes and his mind open will always find
    fitting, though it may be hard schoolmasters, to speed him on
    in his lifelong education."
                    From his *My Schools and Schoolmasters* (1854) xxv.

The Edinburgh Review appears "to erect a higher standard of merit,
and secure a bolder and a purer taste in literature, and to apply
philosophical principles and the maxims of truth and humanity to
politics", 1802.
    "One day we happened to meet in the eighth or ninth storey

or flat in Buccleuch Place, the elevated residence of the then Mr Jeffrey. I proposed that we should get up a Review, and this was acceded to with acclamation.

"I was appointed editor, and remained long enough in Edinburgh to edit the first number of the "Edinburgh Review". The motto I proposed was: *'Tenui musam meditamur avena,* we cultivate literature upon a little oatmeal'. But this was too near the truth to be admitted."

Sydney Smith Preface to his *Works* (1854) 3.

11th

Letter of Andrew de Moray and William Wallace, Generals of the army of Scotland, to the cities of Lübeck and Hamburg, 1297.

"We have learned from trustworthy merchants of Scotland, that you, of your own goodwill, lend your counsel, aid, and favour in all matters touching us and the said merchants; and on that account we are bound to tender you our thanks and to make a worthy return. To do so we willingly engage ourselves to you, requesting that you will make it known among your merchants that they can have safe access to all the ports of the realm of Scotland with their merchandise; for the realm of Scotland, thank God, has been recovered by war from the power of the English."

From the letter in the archives of Lübeck.

13th

St Comgan, 8th century Irish saint, with dedications in Argyll, Lochalsh, and Turriff.

Forward, Scotland's first Socialist weekly, started, 1906.

14th

First steamboat experiment on Dalswinton Loch in Dumfriesshire by Patrick Miller and William Symington, 1788.

"Triple vessels worked by wheels and cranks. . . The steam engine could be applied to work the wheels so to give them a quicker motion, and consequently to increase that of the ship."

From a pamphlet by Miller.

15th

Allan Ramsay, poet, born at Leadhills, 1686.

"Imprimis then, for tallness I am five foot and four inches high; A blackavic'd snod dapper fallow, Nor lean nor over-laid wi tallow. . . Then for the fabric of my mind, 'Tis mair to mirth than grief inclin'd; I rather choose to laugh at folly, Than shew dislike by melancholy. . . I hate a drunkard or a glutton, Yet I'm nae fae to wine and mutton, Proud to be thought a comic poet, And let a judge of numbers know it. . . Well then, I'm nowther Whig nor Tory, Nor credit give to Purgatory; Born to nae lairdship (mair's the pity), Yet denison of this fair city, I make what honest shift I can, And in my ain house, am goodman."

From his *Epistle to James Arbuckle*, January 1719.

King Olav V of Norway in Edinburgh on the first Royal State visit to Scotland since the Union of the Crowns, 1962.

16th

Robert Fergusson, poet, died, 1774.

"No sculptured Marble here, nor pompous Lay,
'No storied Urn nor animated Bust';
This simple Stone directs pale Scotia's Way
To pour her Sorrows o'er her Poet's Dust."

From his tombstone in the Canongate Kirkyard,
set up and thus inscribed by Robert Burns, 1787.

17th

James Young obtains a patent for the extraction of paraffin from shale, the beginning of the paraffin industry in West Lothian, 1850.

"No. 13292. Treating certain bituminous mineral substances; and obtaining products therefrom."

From the Register of Patents.

18th

St Luke's Day. Sour Cakes Day.

"The most famous fair of Rutherglen was St Luke's in October and was signalised by making cakes. About eight or ten days before the fair, a quantity of oatmeal is made into a dough with warm water and laid up in a vessel to ferment."

New Statistical Account of Rutherglen (1836).

20th

Close Season for the killing of hinds ends.

21st

Close season for the killing of stags begins.

23rd

Treaty between King John Balliol of Scotland and King Philippe le Bel of France, made at Paris for mutual military help against the English, "the Auld Alliance", 1295.

"In order that the foresaid injurious efforts may the more conveniently be repressed and that the said king be the more quickly compelled to withdraw from his perverse and hostile incursions, the said king of Scots shall take care to begin and continue war against the king of England at his own cost and expense with all his power and with all the power of his subjects and of his kingdom, as often as it is opportune, while we [the king of France] prosecute and carry on the war which has been begun."

Acts of Parliament Scotland I. 451.

Caledonian Canal opened, 1822, Total length: 60 miles.

"The number of years which this stupendous work has occupied, the vast sums which the munificence of Parliament has expended upon it, and the hopes entertained of the benefits it is calculated to confer on this district, and upon the Empire

at large, have made its successful termination a subject of general congratulation, and of greater public interest than any local event which we can remember."
> *Inverness Courier* 31 Oct.

25th

St Crispin, patron saint of shoemakers, whose incorporations celebrated him by processions and pageants in the various burghs, died, 287.

26th

Death of Lady Caroline Nairne, poetess, at Gask, Perthshire, 1845.

> "I'm wearing awa, John, Like snaw when it's thaw, John,
> I'm wearing awa To the land o the leal.
>
> There's nae sorrow there, John, There's neither cauld nor
>   care, John,
> The day's aye fair In the land o the leal."
>> *To a Friend on the death of her child.*

28th

Battle of Corrichie, defeat and death of the Earl of Huntly in arms against Queen Mary, 1562.

29th

Allan Cunningham, born at Blackwood near Dumfries, 1784, mason, parliamentary reporter, storyteller, biographer, poet, died in London, 1842.
> "It's hame and it's hame, hame fain wad I be,
> And it's hame, hame, hame, to my ain countrie,
> When the flower is i' the bud, and the leaf is on the tree,
> The lark shall sing me hame in my ain countrie."
>> From his *Hame, hame, hame.*

31st

Halloween. All Saints' Eve. The first night of winter when the Celtic year began.

"Halloween is thought to be a night when Witches, Devils, and other mischief-making beings are all abroad on their baneful, midnight errands, particularly those aerial people, the Fairies, are said on that night to hold a grand Anniversary."

Burns *Halloween* note.

NOVEMBER

"November chill blaws loud wi' angry sugh;
  The short'ning winter-day is near a close;
The miry beasts retreating frae the pleugh;
  The black'ning trains o' craws to their repose:
The toil-worn cotter frae his labour goes,
  This night his weary moil is at an end,
Collects his spades, his mattocks and his hoes,
  Hoping the morn in ease and rest to spend,
And weary, o'er the moor, his course does hameward bend."
    Burns *The Cotter's Saturday Night* ii.

Contrive or forecast where and what you are to sow and plant.
Trench and fallow all your vacant grounds. Prepare and mix soils and
composts thoroughly; miss not highway earth, cleansings of streets;
make compositions of manures, soils and lyme.

Lay bair roots of trees that need, and manure such as require it.
Plant all fruit-trees, forrest-trees and shrubs that lose the leaf, also
prune such. Plant cabbage, sow hasties for early peas in warme
grounds, but trust not to them.

Shelter tender evergreen seedlings. House your cabbage, carrots,
turneeps; and at any time ere hard frosts house your potatoes,
parsneeps, etc. Cover asparagus, artichokes, as in the last moneth.
Sow bairs-ears, plant tulips, etc. Shut the conservatory. Preserve your
choisest flowers, Sweep and cleanse the walk of leaves, etc. Stop your
bees close so that you leave breathing vents.

John Reid *The Scots Gard'ner* (1683).

2nd

Patent granted to Nathaniel Udwart of Edinburgh for a monopoly in the manufacture of soap, 1619.

> "Haveing fund his greene soape to be als goode and sufficient as the soape of that kind broght from Flanderis."
>
> From the Privy Council Commission's Report, 1621.

First public meeting of the National Association for the Vindication of Scottish Rights, Edinburgh, 1853.

5th

The Gunpowder Plot to blow up the Houses of Parliament and the members, 1605.

> "When Johnson [Guy Fawkes] was brought to the King's presence, the King asked him how he could conspire so hideous a treason against his children, and so many innocent souls, which never offended him? He answered that it was true; but a dangerous disease required a desperate remedy. He told some of the Scots that his intent was to have blown them back again into Scotland."
>
> Letter from Sir E. Hobart to the British Ambassador at Brussels, Nov. 19, 1605.

Death of James Clerk Maxwell, 1879.

> One of the greatest mathematicians and physicists of the 19th century, born in Edinburgh, 1831, professor at Aberdeen and London, formulated the electro-magnetic theory of light and the kinetic theory of gases, the basis of x-rays and thermo-dynamics, organiser of the Cavendish Laboratory, Cambridge, 1871.

6th

St Leonard, patron saint of Fife, and of prisoners and locksmiths. His hospital at St Andrews became a college in 1512 and part of the University of St Andrews in 1747.

Daniel Stow, founder of Glasgow Normal College for the training
of teachers, pioneer of co-education, opponent of prize-giving and
corporal punishment, died, 1864.

8th

Death of John Duns Scotus, born in Berwickshire, *c.* 1265, scholastic
philosopher at Oxford, Paris and Cologne, 1308.

John of Duns, whose name gave the word *dunce* to the
language, was the opponent of St Thomas Aquinas, in believing
that reason dealt only with the natural world, that faith was
distinct and had to be accepted on authority, and that freewill
was independent of reason. He was noted for the subtlety of
his argumentation.

The first regular public theatre in Scotland opened in Edinburgh,
1736.

"The new theatre in Carrubber's Close, being in great
forwardness, will be opened the first of November. These are
to advertise the Gentlemen and Ladies who incline to purchase
Annual Tickets, to enter their names before the Twentieth of
October next, on which Day they shall receive their tickets
from Allan Ramsay on paying 30s."

Advertisement in the *Caledonian Mercury*, 16 Sept.

9th

The first Co-operative Society in Britain founded by weavers of
Fenwick in Ayrshire, 1769.

"This present Day It is agreed upon by the members of our
Society to take what money we have in our Box and buy what
Victual may be thought Nesessar to sell for the benefit of our
Society. And the mannagers of our society may borrow what
money They think Proper for that End and purpose. And when
the interest is paid of what money you borrow and the men
received their wages for buying and selling thes Victuals we
Deal in the Society will both reap the benefit and sustain the
loss of them."

From the Society's original minute-book.

11th

St Martin's Day, a Scottish Term Day.

> "It fell about the Martinmas, When nichts are lang and mirk,
> The carlin wife's three sons cam hame, And their hats were
>   o the birk."
>   From the ballad *The Wife o Usher's Well*.
> The ghosts of the dead returned to the earth on Martinmas.

12th

St Machar, 5th century, patron saint of Old Aberdeen.

Scottish Staple or entrepôt for trade with the Low Countries established at Middelburg in Zeeland, 1347.

Edinburgh University admits women to the study of medicine, the first in Britain, Sophia Jex-Blake being the first to qualify although not allowed to graduate, 1869. A Dr "James" Barry, a woman who masqueraded as a man and became an army surgeon, actually took a medical degree in Edinburgh in 1812.

13th

St Devenick, 5th century, evangelist in Aberdeenshire and in Caithness and Sutherland, buried at Banchory-Devenick near Aberdeen.

King Malcolm III, "Ceannmor", husband of St Margaret and last of the Celtic Kings of Scotland, killed at the Battle of Alnwick in invading England, 1093.

Battle of Sheriffmuir between the Jacobite army under the Earl of Mar and Hanoverian troops under the Duke of Argyll, 1715.

> "There's some say that we wan And some say that they wan,
>   And some say that nane wan at aa, man;
> But ae thing I'm sure, that at Sheriffmuir

A battle was there that I saw, man;
And we ran, and they ran, and they ran, and we ran
   And we ran, and they ran awa, man."
           From a song on the battle by Rev. Murdoch MacLennan.

Robert Louis Stevenson born in Edinburgh, 1850.
   "I have been a Scotchman all my life and denied my native
land."

   "Give to me the life I love, let the lave go by me,
   Give the jolly heaven above And the byway nigh me.
   Let the blow fall soon or late, Let what will be o'er me,
   Give the face of earth around, And the road before me."
           From his *Songs of Travel*.

16th

Margaret, Queen of Malcolm Canmore, grand-niece of Edward the
Confessor, exiled in Scotland after William the Conqueror's
invasion, introduced English influence into the Scottish Church,
died, 1093. She had a chapel in Edinburgh Castle, was buried in
Dunfermline, and was canonised in 1251.

James MacPherson, a freebooter, hanged at Banff, 1700. The town
clock was said to have been advanced to forestall a reprieve. He
played his fiddle up to the last.

   "Farewell, ye dungeons dark and strong, The wretch's destinie!
   McPherson's time will not be long On yonder gallows-tree.
   Sae rantingly, sae wantonly, Sae dantonly gaed he;
   He play'd a spring and danced it round, Below the gallows-tree."
           Burns *McPherson's Farewell*.

17th

Death of Thomas Erskine, born 1750, advocate, defender of Lord
George Gordon, Thomas Paine and other radicals, and of Queen
Caroline, Whig Politician, Lord Chancellor, 1806-7, died, 1823.
   "Lord Erskine, however hard pressed, was no man to fear either
the court or king or the king's judges, but he did his duty to his

client in spite of all that power held out to intimidate or tempt
him."

> Brougham on Erskine, 1864.

18th

St Fergus, 6th century, evangelist in Strathearn, Angus, Aberdeenshire and Caithness, with dedications at Wick, Halkirk, Dyce and St
Fergus near Peterhead.

19th

Charles I born at Dunfermline Palace, 1600.

20th

Death of the first Viscount of Stair, 1695.

> James Dalrymple, Covenanter, professor at Glasgow Univer-
> sity, Lord President, opposed the Test Acts and fled to
> Holland, supporter of William of Orange, best known for his
> masterly systematising of Scots Law in his *Institutions of the Law
> of Scotland*, 1681.

21st

Bull of Pope Honorius III, affirming the independence of the
Church of Scotland, 1218.

> "We by the present writing following the example of our
> predecessors of happy memory, Celestine and Innocent,
> Roman Pontiffs, strictly charge that seeing the Scottish Church
> is subject to the Apostolic see as a special daughter, it be lawful
> to no one except the Roman Pontiff or a Legate sent *de latere*,
> to publish sentence of interdict or excommunication in the
> kingdom of Scotland . . ."

> From the Latin of the Bull.

James Hogg, the Ettrick Shepherd, died at Altrive in Yarrow, 1835.

"When many a day had come and fled,
When grief grew calm and hope was dead,

When mass for Kilmeny's soul had been sung,
When the bedesman had prayed and the dead-bell rung,
Late, late in a gloamin when all was still,
When the fringe was red on the westlin hill,
The wood was sere, the moon i' the wane,
The reek o' the cot hung ower the plain,
Like a wee red cloud in the world its lane;
When the ingle lowed with an eiry leme,
Late, late in the gloamin Kilmeny came hame."
     From his *Queen's Wake.*

22nd

St Cecilia, patron saint of music. First recorded public concert in Edinburgh, 1695.

The order of instruments was 7 first violins, 5 second violins, 6 flutes, 2 oboes, 1 harpsichord, 5 cellos, 5 viol de gambos. The programme included motets of Bussoni and a sonata of Corelli.

24th

Battle of Solway Moss and defeat of the Scots by an English cavalry force under Lord Dacre, 1545.

"Quhan the King of Scotland saw that his lordis wald on na wayes pleiss to pass forward. . . he caussit to make ane proclamatioun in the midis of the airmie and made Olipheir Sincklar ane of his fameliear servandis lufetennent ower the said airmie. . . bot the lordis and nobilitie seand the kingis willful misgovernance towart his awin common weill of Scotland and wald not use thair consall thairunto, consultit togither and said they wald on na wayis fight under Oliepheir Sincklaris banner ffor they knew him nocht for no governour nor yeit lutennent to thame and concludit haill in ane purpois that they had lever be taine and had to Ingland to King Hary nor to bide the kingis furie in Scotland or tyranne wroght on thame be consall of the preistis and courteouris. . . and so be this unhappie chance and misgovernance of the Scottismen thair was money of them taine and had to Ingland as pressoneris."
     Pitscottie *Croniclis* XXI. xxxviii.

John Knox died, 1572.

"About five houres he sayeth to his wife, 'Goe, read where I cast my first anker,' and so she read the 17th chapter of the Gospell according to Johne, and after that, some sermons of Mr Calvin's upon the Ephesians. About half houre to tenne, they went to the ordinar prayer, which being ended, Doctor Preston said unto him, 'Sir heard yee the prayer?' He answered, 'I would to God that yee and all men heard them as I heard; I praise God for that heavenlie sound.' "

D. Calderwood *Historie of the Kirk* III. 237.

25th

Commission from Charles II to Sir Thomas Dalyell of the Binns to form a regiment of horse, the Royal Regiment of Scots Dragoons, later the Royal Scots Grays, originally for the suppression of the Covenanters, 1681.

"The Scots Greys came up at this moment, and doubling round our [Gordon Highlanders'] flanks and through our centre where openings were made for them, both Regiments charged together, calling out 'Scotland for ever.' "

H.T. Siborne *Waterloo Letters* (1891) 393.

26th

John Loudoun MacAdam, born in Ayr 1756, Surveyor-General of Roads in Britain, 1824, died at Moffat, 1836. His name survives in the words *macadamise* and *tarmac*.

"Every road is to be made of broken stone without mixture of earth or any other matter; no large stones to be employed on pretence of bottoming, nor any sand, earth or other matter on pretence of binding."

From his report to the Select Committee on Highways, 1810-11.

27th

Death of Andrew Meikle, inventor of the threshing-machine, 1811.

"His father, James, built the first barley mill in Scotland and the
first winnowing machine. . . He died at Houston Mill, East
Lothian, at the age of 92, having given to the world of agriculture
one of its most essential pieces of machinery."
> A. Fenton *Scottish Country Life* (1976) 84.

28th

Battle of Rullion Green and defeat of the Covenanters by Sir
Thomas Dalyell, 1666.

"Blows the wind today, and the sun and the rain are flying,
> Blows the wind on the moors today and now,

Where about the graves of the martyrs the whaups are crying,
> My heart remembers how!

Be it granted to me to behold you again in dying,
> Hills of home! and to hear again the call;

Hear about the graves of the martyrs the peewees crying,
> And hear no more at all."
>> From R.L. Stevenson *To S.R. Crockett.*

29th

The Solemn League and Covenant between England and Scotland
signed, 1643.
> "As a most near tye and conjunction betwixt them, for their
> mutual defence against the papist and prelatical faction, and their
> adherents in both kingdoms.'
>> From the first article in the treaty.

Royal College of Physicians, Edinburgh, granted their charter by
Charles II, 1681.
> "I, having recovered ane warrand of King James the sixt, of
> happie memorie, derected to the Commissioner and Estaits of
> Parliament, then sitting in Scotland, dated the 3rd of July, 1621,
> with ane reference by the Parliament thereanent, to the Lords of
> Secret Counsell, with power to doe therein what they thought
> fitt, produced this to his Royall Highness [James, Duke of York]

who, so soon as he saw it superscribed by King James, said with much satisfaction, he knew his grandfather's hand, and he would see our byseness done, and from that moment acted vigorously for us, so that it was resolved there sould be ane colledge of Physitians, butt it took a long tyme of dispute befor the Counsell in answering the objections of the Chirurgeons and of the Town of Edinburgh against it."

Sir Robert Sibbald, M.D. *Autobiography*.

30th

St. Andrew's Day. Patron saint of Scotland from the ninth century.

"Now on the next day it happened that the said king was walking with seven of his dearest comrades when a divine light shone around them and they, unable to endure it, fell to the earth on their faces and behold, a voice from Heaven was heard: 'Angus, Angus, listen to me, the apostle of Christ, Andrew, who am sent to defend and guard thee, but behold the sign of the cross of Christ, which is set in the sky and marches forward against thine enemies. But offer up a tenth part of thine inheritance as a share and offering to Almighty God, and in honour of His saint, Andrew.'

On the third day he divided his army into twelve companies, and the sign of the cross preceded each one; and a divine light shone from the head of each sign. And they were victorious."

From the legend of St Andrew in Skene's *Chronicles of the Picts and Scots* No. 18.

Angus, King of the Picts and Scots, reigned from 820-834.

First international association football match between Scotland and England, in Glasgow, 1872. The result was a goalless draw.

DECEMBER

"When biting Boreas, fell and doure,
Sharp shivers thro' the leafless bower,
When Phoebus gies a short-lived glower
    Far south the lift,
Dim-darkening thro' the flaky shower,
    Or whirling drift.

Ae night the storm the steeples rocked,
Poor labour sweet in sleep was locked,
While burns, wi' snawy wreaths up-chocked,
    Wild-eddying swirl,
Or thro' the mining outlet bocked
    Down headlong hurl.

Listening the doors an' winnocks rattle,
I thought me on the ourie cattle,
Or silly sheep wha bide this brattle
    O' winter war,
And thro' the drift deep-lairing sprattle
    Beneath a scaur.

Ilk happing bird, wee helpless thing,
That in the merry months o' spring,
Delighted me to hear thee sing,
    What comes o' thee?

> Where wilt thou cower thy chittering wing,
> An' close thy ee?"
> Burns *A Winter Night.*

Trench and prepare grounds. Gather together composts; plant trees in nurseries, and sow their seeds that endure it.

Continue your care in preserving choice carnations, anemonies, and ranunculuses from raines and frosts. And keep the greenhouse close against the piercing colds. Turne and refresh your fruit in a clear serene day. Sharpen and mend tools. Cover your water pipes with leitter lest the frosts do crack them; feed weak bees.

John Reid *The Scots Gard'ner* (1683).

The *Encyclopedia Britannica* first appeared in parts from Dec. 1768, edited by William Smellie.

"Encyclopedia Britannica or a Dictionary of Arts and Sciences compiled upon a New Plan, in which the different Sciences and Arts are digested into distinct treatises or Systems, and the various Technical Terms, etc., are explained as they occur in the order of the Alphabet. Illustrated with One Hundred and Sixty Copperplates. By a Society of Gentlemen in Scotland. In Three Volumes. Edinburgh. Printed by A. Bell and C. Macfarquhar and sold by Colin Macfarquhar at his Printing Office, Nicolson Street. MDCCLXXI."

From the title-page.

1st

The first lighthouse in Scotland, built at Kinnaird Head, Fraserburgh, by Thomas Smith and Robert Stevenson, lit, 1787.

2nd

Mary Slessor, a mill-girl in Dundee, trained as a missionary for the United Presbyterian Church and worked against savage folk-rites and to improve conditions for negro women in Calabar, Nigeria, where she died in 1915, born in Aberdeen, 1848.

"By her enthusiasm, self-sacrifice and greatness of character she has earned the devotion of thousands of the natives among whom she worked, and the love and esteem of all Europeans

irrespective of class or creed, with whom she came in contact.'
From an obituary in the Government *Gazette*.

3rd

Signing of the Common or Godly Band by the Earls of Argyll,
Glencairn and Morton and others, the "Lords of the Congregation",
the first manifesto of the Reformation in Scotland, 1557.

"We persaving how Sathan in his membris the Antechristes of
oure tyme, crewellie dois Raige seiking to downethring and to
destroye the Evangell of Christ and his Congregatioune, awght
according to our bownden dewtys to stryve in oure maisteres
Cawss, even unto the deth, Being certane of the victorye in
Him. The quhilk our dewtie being weill consyderit, we do
promis before the Majestie of God, and his congregatioune,
that we be his grace sall with all diligence continewallie applie
oure hoill power, substannce and oure very lyves to mentene
sett forward and establische the maist blissed worde of God
and his Congregatioune."

Robert Louis Stevenson, poet and novelist, died at Vailima in Samoa,
1894.
"Under the wide and starry sky Dig the grave and let me lie,
Glad did I live and gladly die, And I laid me down with a will.

This be the verse you grave for me—'Here he lies where he
    longed to be;
Home is the sailor, home from sea, And the hunter home from
    the hill.' "
From his own *Requiem*.

4th

William Drummond of Hawthornden, poet and scholar, author of
sonnets and madrigals, *The Cypress Grove, Polemo-middinia,* etc., died,
1649.

"Thrice happie hee, who by some shadie Grove,
Farre from the clamorous World, doth live his owne,

Though solitarie, who is not alone,
But doth converse with that Eternall Love:
O! how more sweete is Birds harmonious Moane,
Or the hoarse Sobbings of the widow'd Dove,
Than those smooth whisperings neere a Princes Throne,
Which Good make doubtfull, doe the evill approve?
O! how more sweet is Zephires wholesome Breath,
And Sighes embalm'd, which new-borne Flowrs unfold,
Than that applause vaine Honour doth bequeath?
How sweete are Streames to poison drunke in Gold?
The World is full of Horrours, Troubles, Slights,
Woods harmelesse Shades have only true Delightes."
The Praise of a Solitarie Life.

5th

Sir Robert Watson Watt, born in Brechin 1892, graduate in Science of St Andrews University, inventor of radar, died, 1973.

"So rewarding were his efforts in that sphere [radar], which quickly flourished and provided 'electronic eyes' for night fighter and bomber aircraft and Allied ships at sea, that the German High Command ultimately recognised radar as the greatest single device, even including the atom bomb, that brought total victory to the Allies."

From his obituary in *The Times*, 7 Dec.

6th

St Nicholas, patron saint of Aberdeen, celebrated in the Middle Ages by pageants and mummery, died, 342.

"The provoist, bailyies, etc. of the said burgh in the honour of thar glorious patronn Saint Nicholas, statut and ordaint that all persons habill to rid, to decor and honor the towne, sall rid with Robert Huyd and Litile Johne, quhilk was callit yers bypast Abbot and Prior of Bon Accord, on every Saint Nicholas day."

Council Register of Aberdeen, 17 Nov. 1508.

Lady Grisell Baillie, born 1665, poetess, noted for having concealed her father, Sir Patrick Hume, Earl of Marchmont, a Covenanter, from his persecutors, for over a month in the family vault of Polwarth Kirk in 1685, died, 1746.

"When bonnie young Johnie cam over the sea,
He vow'd he saw naething sae lovely as me;
He gae me gowd rings, and mony braw things,
An' were na my heart licht I wad dee . . .

O, were we young now as we ance hae been,
We should hae been galloping down on yon green,
And linking it o'er the lily-white lea,
An' were na my heart licht I wad dee."
        From her song *Were na my heart licht.*

8th

King James V, father of Mary, Queen of Scots, died at Falkland Palace, 1542.
    "Be this the post came out of Lythgow schawing to the King goode tydingis that the quene was deliverit. The King inquyrit 'wither it was man or woman'. The messenger said 'it was ane fair douchter'. The King ansuerit and said, 'Adew, fair weill, it come with ane lase, it will pas with ane lase,' and so he recommendit himself to the marcie of Almightie God and spak ane lyttill then frome that tyme fourth, bot turnit his bak unto his lordis and his face into the wall."
        Pitscottie *Croniclis* XXI. xxxix.

10th

Ordinance for Parish Schools, 1616.
    "The Kingis Majestie, with advise of the Lordis of his Secreit Counsall, hes thocht it necessar and expedient that in everie parroche of this Kingdome whair convenient meanes may be had for interteyning a scoole, that a scoole salbe establisheit, upoun the expensis of the parrochinneris.
        Register of the Privy Council X. 671.
    This had been approved by the General Assembly in 1562.

The same act of the Privy Council unfortunately commended the abolition of Gaelic.

Death of Duncan Forbes of Culloden, Lord President of the Court of Session, who was largely responsible for the failure of the Jacobite Rising 1745-6 and tried to mitigate the subsequent repressive measures, 1747.

Charles Rennie Mackintosh, born 1868, leader of the Art Nouveau movement, architect of the Glasgow School of Art, Cranston's Tea-rooms, and other buildings in and around Glasgow, died, 1928.

12th

Sir James MacGregor, Dean of Lismore, Vicar of Fortingall, compiler of the oldest collection of Gaelic poetry, 1551.

> "Na biodh anns an domhan-sa do shagart na do thuathach
> 'ga bhfuil ni 'na gcomhghar-san nach cuirther e san Duanair."
> (Let there not be in this world one priest or layman who has anything at his hand that is not put in the Song-book).
> From Finlay MacNab *Duanaire na sracaire.*

14th

St Drostan, founder of the Celtic Abbey of Deer, 6th century.
> "Columcille [Columba] and Drostan, son of Cosgrach his pupil, came from I [Iona] as God had shown to them unto Aberdour and Bede the Pict was mormaer of Buchan before them, and it was he that gave them that town in freedom for ever from mormaer and tosech. . . Drostan's tears [deara] came on parting with Columcillie. Said Columcille 'Let Dear be its name henceforward'."
> From the Gaelic of the *Book of Deer*, the oldest Celtic MS. of Scotland.

The University of Stirling constituted by Royal Charter, 1967.

17th

Baptism of King James VI at Stirling, 1566.

> "The prince was bapteist, and namet Charles James, on this maneir. The said prince was borne out of his chalmer to the chappell be the Frenche ambassadour, my ladie of Ergyle, cummer for the quene of England, be commissioun, and Monsieur Lacrok for the duke of Savoy, . . . and at the chappell dore the prince was ressavit be my lord of Sanctandrois, quha was executour officii in pontificalibus, with staf, mytoure, croce, and the rest . . . The said prince was bapteist in the said font, and thir solempnities endit be neir fyve houris eftirnone, with singing and playing on organis. At this tyme my lordis Huntlie, Murray, Bothwill, nor the Inglis ambassatour come nocht within the said chappell, becaus it was done against the poyntis of thair religioun."
>
> *Diurnal of Occurrents.*

Death of William Thomson, Lord Kelvin, mathematician, physicist, engineer, professor of Natural Philosophy at Glasgow, 1846-99, devised the absolute temperature scales, inventor in cable-signalling, developed the law of conservation of energy and the theory of thermodynamics, 1907.

18th

The "Elizabeth" of Burntisland lost off the English coast with the Scottish records aboard, being returned from London, to which they had been taken by Cromwell, 1661.

> "The humble petitione of Johne Wemys, late Master of the shippe callit the Elizabeth sheweth that it is not unknowne how the petitioners shippe with all the goods therein was lately lost at sea be no defect on the petitioners pairt. Bot being mistrimmed by 85 hogsheads of Registars and papers violently putt therein against the petitioners consent in Yarmouth roads quhairby the leck could not be found out."
>
> From the Petition of John Wemyss to Parliament, 20 March.

The Society of Antiquaries of Scotland founded, 1780.

"In the year 1780, your petitioners, consisting of a number of the Noblemen and Gentlemen of this part of Your Majesty's United Kingdom, formed themselves into a Society for investigating antiquities as well as natural and civil history in general, with a view to the improvement of the minds of mankind, and to promote a taste for natural and useful knowledge."

From the Society's Petition for a Royal Charter, 1782.

20th

First General Assembly of the Kirk met in Edinburgh, 1560.

21st

Death of Sir John Sinclair of Ulbster, M.P., President of the Board of Agriculture, organiser of the first Statistical Account of Scotland, 1835.

"It is now about twelve months since I first had the honour of circulating among the clergy of the Church of Scotland a variety of queries for the purpose of elucidating the Natural History and Political State of that country. My original idea was to have drawn up from their returns a general Statistical View of North Britain without any reference to Parochial districts. But I found such merit and ability and so many useful facts and important observations in the answers which were sent me, that I could not think of depriving the Clergy of the credit they were entitled to derive from such laborious exertions."

From the preface of the First Statistical Account, 1795.

22nd

Prince James Francis Stewart, "The Old Pretender", lands at Peterhead, 1715.

"His Person is tall and thin, seeming to encline to be lean rather than to fill as he grows in Years. His Countenance is pale. . . yet he seems to be sanguine in his Constitution, and has something of a Vivacity in his Eye that perhaps would have been more visible if he had not been under dejected Circumstances and surrounded with Discouragement. His

Speech was grave and not very clearly expressing his Thoughts, nor overmuch to the Purpose."
From *A True Account of the Proceedings at Perth*,
9 Jan. 1716.

23rd

St Mayota, one of the nine daughters of St Donald (see 12 July), 8th century, with a dedication at Drumoak.

24th

Christmas Eve. Yule Een. The beginning of the Daft Days.
"When merry Yule-day comes, I trow,
You'll scantlins find a hungry mou;
Sma' are our cares, our stamacks fou
        O' gusty gear,
And kickshaws, strangers to our view,
        Sin fairn-year."
        Fergusson *The Daft Days* (1772).

General George Wade appointed Commander-in-Chief in Scotland, 1724, after his report on the need for military roads in Scotland.
"If you had seen these roads before they were made,
You would hold up your hands and bless General Wade."
        Anon.

25th

Christmas Day. Yule.
"And it was done, quhile thai ware thar, the dais ware fulfillit that scho suld beire childe.

And scho baire hire first born sonn and wrappit him in clathis, and laid him in a cribbe; for there was na place to him in na chalmere.

And schephirdis war in the samin cuntre wakand and kepand the wacheingis of the nycht on thare flock.

And lo, the angel of the Lorde stude beside thame, and the

cleirnes of God schynit about thame; and thai dredd with gret dreed.

And the angel said to thame, Will ye nocht dreed; for lo, I preche to you a gret joy that sal be to all the pepile.

For a salvatour is born this day to you, that is Crist the Lord, in the citee of David.

And this is a takin to you: ye sall find a young child wlappit in clathis and laid in a cribbe.

And suddanlie there was made with the angel a multitude of hevenlie knichthede loving God, and sayand,

Glorie be in the hieast thingis to God, and in erd pece, to men off gude will."

> Murdoch Nisbet *New Testament* Luke ii. 6-14 (*c.* 1520).

St Bathan, with dedications in Berwickshire and East Lothian, died, *c.* 639.

The Scottish Coronation Stone removed from Westminster Abbey, 1950.

"One man holding the torch, one prising at the sides with the jemmy, and one pushing at the back, we started afresh. It moved. It slid forward. We had moved the Stone. The English Chair would hold it no longer."

> Ian Hamilton, *No Stone Unturned* 82.

26th

Sweetie Scone Day.

"In Scotland there is a custom of distributing sweet-cakes and a particular kind of sugared bread before and after the New Year."

> *Gentleman's Magazine*, July 1790.

Commission to the Marquess of Atholl to raise 'the Highland Host' against the Covenanters, 1677.

"We doe hereby impower and requyre John, Marquis of Atholl, to convocat and draw together the gentlemen and heretours of the shyre of Perth who are to march under his command on horseback, and to convocat and raise the

Highlanders in the countrey of Atholl and to forme them in regiments, troupes and companies, as he shall think fitt. . . and wee herby indemnifie them against all persuits, civill and criminall which may at any tyme hereafter be intented against them for any thing they shall doe in our service by killing, wounding, apprehending or imprisoning such as shall make opposition to our authority or by seizing such as they have reason to suspect."

Register of the Privy Council V. 301.

28th

Robert MacGregor or Campbell, of Inversnaid, Highland gentleman, freebooter and outlaw, died at Balquhidder, 1734.

"Rob Roy, though a kittle neighbour to the Low Country, and particularly obnoxious to his Grace [the Duke of Montrose] and though he maybe carried the cateran trade farther than ony man o' his day, was an auld-farrand carle, and there might be some means found of making him hear reason; whereas his wife and sons were reckless fiends, without either fear or mercy about them, and at the head of a' his limmer louns, would be a worse plague to the country than ever he had been."

Sir Walter Scott *Rob Roy* xxxii.

The first Tay Railway Bridge blown down in a storm while a train was passing over it with 78 passengers and crew, and the consequent loss of all lives, 1879.

"It continued its way onwards, entered the high girders in the middle of the Bridge, and when just about to emerge from them at the north end, a fearful blast, with a noise like thunder, swept down the river. At that moment two intensely brilliant sheets of flame and showers of sparks were seen to rise from the high girders, evidently resulting from the friction of the ponderous ironwork as it crashed and tumbled into the river below from the horrible height of about 100 feet. Simultaneously with the disappearance of the sparks and flashes of light the train also disappeared; and before they had time to realise their fearful position, the whole of the 200 passengers were ushered into eternity."

Dundee Courier and Argus, Monday, 29 December 1879.

31st

Hogmanay. Gaelic Oidhche Chaluinne.

From the French dialect *hoguinané*, French *aguillanneuf*, a song sung by children going from door to door for New Year gifts. In Scotland the song goes thus:

> "Get up, guidwife, and shak your feathers,
> And dinna think that we are beggars,
> For we are bairns come out to play,
> Get up and gie's our Hogmanay."

On First-footing:

"The first-fit generally carries with him a hot beverage, made of ale, spirits, eggs, cream, sugar, and biscuit, with some slices of curran bun to be eaten along with it, or perhaps some bread and cheese."

E. Picken *Dictionary of the Scottish Language* (1818).